MODI AND MARKETS

MODI AND MARKETS

ARGUMENTS FOR TRANSFORMATION

Dhiraj Nayyar

First published by Westland Publications Private Limited in 2018
61, 2nd Floor, Silverline Building, Alapakkam Main Road, Maduravoyal, Chennai 600095

Westland and the Westland logo are the trademarks of Westland Publications Private Limited, or its affiliates.

ISBN: 9789387578852

10 9 8 7 6 5 4 3 2 1

Typeset by Ram Das Lal, New Delhi, NCR
Printed at Manipal Technologies Limited, Manipal

For my parents,
Rohini & Deepak Nayyar

CONTENTS

Modi

Markets

FOREWORD

In the twenty-first century, success for individuals, firms, governments and even nations will be defined by the ability to create and innovate. Without creativity, innovation and risk, which are amongst the chief characteristics of entrepreneurship—there is only stagnation. Seventy years after Independence, after several steps forward and perhaps some backward, India is finally on the threshold of taking a giant leap to achieve its unrealised, but very real potential.

The lead actor in India's long journey of development is the government. No country has ever advanced without a strong government at the helm. Unfortunately in India, the government hasn't always got its role right. It has acted too strongly in areas which are best left to the private sector, like running businesses for example. It has acted too meekly in areas which need determined government action, like education, health, nutrition, or the building of world-class infrastructure.

The government of Prime Minister Modi has made strenuous efforts to change that scenario. His government has taken several steps to carry out reforms. On the one hand, there is an ongoing exercise to get the government to do less in certain areas, thereby unleashing the powerful engine of market forces. For instance, the task of cutting red tape and making the environment easier and simpler for private enterprise has already borne fruit with India's rank in the World Bank's Ease of Doing Business survey improving by forty-two positions during Modi's tenure. There has also been an attempt to make the processes trouble-free in the states, and have them compete on various indicators. This has resulted in inculcating a fierce competitive spirit amongst them.

Additionally, a radical liberalisation of rules governing Foreign Direct Investment (FDI) across an entire gamut of sectors, including the previously untouched Defence sector, has also come to fruition. It is to the credit of this dispensation that the moribund strategic disinvestment programme has got a new lease of life—several terminally-sick public sector companies have been closed down. In order to guarantee private sector's growth, there's been a strong commitment towards fiscal discipline, and maintaining a stable macro-economy.

On a different track, the government has brought greater efficiency to the tasks it must continue to perform. Prime Minister Modi has adopted the power of technology and harnessed the principle of competition, usually associated with the private sector, to reinvent governance. For the first time in India's post-Independent history, there is an intensive monitoring of flagship government-run programmes. The Prime Minister took the lead with the PRAGATI video-conferencing with Secretaries and Chief Secretaries of states to find solutions for projects which were either stalled, or delayed indefinitely. Through twenty-five meetings via video-conferencing, Narendra Modi succeeded in clearing over 227 projects worth more than 10.5 lakh crores.

The Finance ministry, along with the NITI Aayog, is working on the outcome budgets of all ministries—for the first time ever, each ministry is held acountable for the money allocated to them.

The government has also enabled the JAM Trinity or Jan Dhan Aadhaar Mobile Phone combination to cut wastage in benefit transfers to the poor and deposit money into the bank accounts of those who need it most.

There is a genuine attempt to establish that the Narendra Modi-led government is not just an entity which rules in New Delhi, but also one which operates in India's twenty-nine states, and over 700 districts.

This idea basically stems from the prime minister's initiative of fusing both cooperative and competitive federalism into the governance structures of India. It is Modi's strong belief that the three tiers of government—Centre, state and local—must work as a team, but they should also be intensely competitive and learn from best shared practices.

The NITI Aayog ranks the states on their performance in crucial sectors like education, health and water, so that there is sufficient pressure on the governments to perform as per established norms.

The 115 Aspirational Districts Programme (ADP), which was launched by Prime Minister Modi in January 2018, employs the principles of cooperative and competitive federalism across forty-nine indicators to uplift India's most backward regions on parametres such as, education, health, farming, infrastructure, financial inclusion, and skills.

It is easy to be both sceptical and cynical, but there is a well-thought out mechanism in the way the government is going about fulfilling its mission. In what is yet another radical and extremely significant step, the government is also acting firmly against corruption and crony capitalism which in the past have brought disrepute to both the country and particularly the private sector, while undermining the legitimacy of the market economy.

India has a long list of entrepreneurs who have created wealth most honestly, and several began with little or no capital while establishing their enterprise. There is no doubt that India, more than ever before, has one of the most vibrant ecosystems for start-ups. The government encourages every small to medium entrepreneur to strike out on their own and the results are apparent for large numbers who are not only excelling in e-commerce, but across health, agriculture, education, and social innovation. Ultimately, only a vibrant private sector can generate jobs and provide opportunities for India's youth. Markets are the key to prosperity.

This book, which is a collection of some brilliant articles by Dhiraj Nayyar, succinctly captures the transformation that is taking place in India. As Officer on Special Duty in NITI Aayog, with charge of the Economics, Finance and Trade verticals, Dhiraj has a vantage point in seeing some of these changes up-close. He is one amongst several young persons that NITI Aayog hired from outside the government to bring in a fresh perspective and infuse new energy to the business of government. I am delighted that he has been writing about the changes and reforms and congratulate him on this book, which I hope will be widely read.

Meanwhile, the work to transform India continues—unabated with a lot of creativity, plenty of innovation and constructive competition.

Amitabh Kant
CEO, NITI Aayog
New Delhi, August 2018

ACKNOWLEDGEMENTS

This book represents a body of work put together over a decade. Needless to say, many persons have played an influential role in shaping my journey as a thinker and writer over this long period.

At the outset, I would like to thank the late Professor Ajit Singh, my doctoral supervisor at the University of Cambridge who always encouraged my non-academic writing and fully supported a radical move away from the ivory tower to the real world of journalism. They don't make people like Ajit anymore.

I owe a debt of gratitude to all my mentors and bosses in journalism.

Shekhar Gupta, then Editor-in-Chief of *The Indian Express* for giving me my first job in journalism, also my first assignment of responsibility as Editor of the Opinion Pages of *The Financial Express* at the young age of thirty-one and plenty of column space to express my views. At the *Express*, Saubhik Chakrabarti and M.K. Venu were always generous with their praise, and gentle with criticism.

M.J. Akbar, then Editorial Director of *India Today*, for introducing me to the wonderful and curiosity-filled world of reportage. He is the most brilliant mentor for a young journalist.

Aroon Purie, Editor-in-Chief of *India Today*, for his wisdom, sagacity and support. The media needs more proprietors like AP. Kaveree Bamzai, then Editor of *India Today*, for always keeping a lookout.

Raghav Bahl, then of Network 18, for bringing me into the digital century, always complimenting a good argument whether he agreed with it or not, and for letting me anchor a television show! R. Jagannathan and Durga Raghunath were exemplary at *Firstpost*. What an exhilarating time it was.

David Shipley and Nisid Hajari of *Bloomberg View* for taking my views to a global audience with much added sophistication. A superb writer himself, Nisid taught me the value of a good edit. At *The Sunday Guardian*, M.D. Nalapat and Joyeeta Basu for including me in an exceptional cast of veteran commentators.

Over the years, regardless of where I have worked, I owe a very special debt of gratitude to S. Prasannarajan and Mini Kapoor. Thank you for the friendship. I name you both partners-in-crime for this book. Many of the ideas expressed in it have been born out of conversations in the office and outside.

Veenu Sandal, friend, philosopher, guide. Words are not enough.

Rajesh Jain and Parth Shah, champions of free markets, for inspiration.

I would also like to thank the following friends and colleagues for their insights: Surjit S. Bhalla, Bharat Lal, Ashok Malik, Sadanand Dhume, Subhomoy Bhattacharjee, Sunil Jain, Renuka Bisht, P. Raghavan, Jaya Jumrani, Vandita Mishra, Mihir Sharma, Amulya Gopalakrishnan, Vinay Sitapati, Priya Sahgal, Sandeep Unnithan, S. Sahaya Ranjit, Gayatri Jayaraman and Vaishna Roy.

In 2015, my career took an unexpected turn when I was invited to work for the government at the NITI Aayog as Officer on Special Duty and Head of Economics, Finance and Commerce. I would like to sincerely thank Professor Arvind Panagariya and Professor Bibek Debroy for giving me this unique opportunity, and Dr Rajiv Kumar for keeping the faith. Their wise leadership has deftly guided NITI Aayog through a period of transition from the old Planning Commission.

I would also like to thank Amitabh Kant, CEO of NITI Aayog who has been an inspiration. If more IAS officers were like him, India would have been transformed.

At NITI Aayog, I would like to thank all my colleagues. In particular, Y.S. Malik, Anil K. Jain and Alok Kumar for the discussions on the intricacies of government; Rahul Ahluwalia, Pavithra Rangan, Kishore Desai and Suparna Jain, fellow outsiders, we discovered government together; Atisha Kumar, Chinmaya Goyal, Ranveer Nagaich, Urvashi Prasad, Devashish Dhar and Vaibhav Kapoor for being an excellent team to mentor and for the ideation on any number of policy issues. This book is much richer from my experience in government.

My biggest gratitude is reserved for my home base. My parents have been my staunchest supporters for forty years, through ups and downs. They presented me those priceless gifts of nature and nurture. No thank you would suffice. My parents-in-law, Veena and Upendra Arora, lovers of books, makers of books. I hope this will adorn your shelves. I probably would not have dabbled in writing full time without the support and encouragement of my wife, Divya. The list of things I need to thank her for would run into the length of a book. She knows. Our dog, Dali, has sat patiently by my side as I have written many of these articles. He has also taught me a lot about life. Thank you, my friend. My man Friday, Ram Kumar for the unending supply of nimbu pani and chicken kababs which nourished my writing.

I would like to sincerely thank *The Hindu, Open, Bloomberg View, The Sunday Guardian, Firstpost.com, The Indian Express, The Financial Express, India Today, The Economic Times, East Asia Forum, Economic and Political Weekly,* and *DNA* for permission to republish articles that were originally written for these brilliant news outlets.

And finally, thank you Sudha Sadhanand for being a most patient publisher. Apologies for the missed deadlines and gratitude for making this happen.

Dhiraj Nayyar
August 2018

INTRODUCTION

Four years ago, when Narendra Modi was sworn in as India's sixteenth prime minister in May 2014, India's economic rise was at an inflexion point. Between 1991 and 2004, successive governments of different political colours had maintained a momentum in favour of pro-market liberalisation. Their efforts, combined with a boom in the global economy in the first half of the 2000s, reaped rich dividends for India which attained almost double-digit growth per annum in the years between 2003 and 2012. Finally, India seemed to have acquired the ability to grow at the levels of East Asia. But it was not going to last.

For one, the liberalisation that happened between 1991 and 2004 largely focused on product markets in manufacturing and services. There was no reform in two crucial factor markets, land and labour, and limited reform in the third factor market, capital. While equity markets were liberalised in the 1990s, the banking system and debt markets remained stuck in the past. Agriculture was completely bypassed by market reform. An incomplete reform agenda awaited the UPA government that was elected to office in 2004. Unfortunately, in the aftermath of the Atal Bihari Vajpayee-led NDA's failed India Shining campaign, and the huge influence of the Communist parties in the UPA-I government, market reform took a back seat while old-fashioned populism of big government spending took centre stage. The global boom and access to cheap finance lulled the policy machinery into a sense of complacency. If the economy was growing at near double-digits with the status quo, where was the need for pro-market reform.

* * *

Since 1991, there was always very little conviction and openness about the need for market reform across the political spectrum. Market reform in India had been necessitated by an acute balance of payments crisis and not a fundamental change in the conviction of the broader political economy. Most reform was carried out by stealth in the fear that market reform would be seen as pro-rich or pro-business in a country that was still low income. From 2004 onwards, forget conviction, even necessity seemed irrelevant. At some point, the abandonment of further reform would return to bite.

The global economic crisis of 2008 should have served as an early warning sign. The steroids that were keeping the Indian economy in high growth mode would soon become unavailable as the advanced economies lurched from what began as a crisis in the private sector to sovereign debt crises (most notably in the infamous PIGS economies) in what would become a 'lost decade' for some parts of the West. In India, a narrative was built that prudent economic policies had saved the country from the worst effects of the crisis. Market reform, particularly of the financial sector, was something to be eschewed. Capitalism was destroying its home countries, so why should India embrace it? A political class that was always shy of market reform found one more reason to ignore it. In fact, the crisis of 2008 was an opportunity to reaffirm the wisdom of statist policies.

Perhaps no one would still have predicted how spectacularly the Indian growth story would collapse in 2012, especially after the economy seemed to have weathered the global storm. But there were serious side effects of the remarkable growth story of the 2000s.

The most serious was the unleashing of a most virulent strain of crony capitalism. An economy where the government still retained swathes of control across diverse sectors was always vulnerable to this. The virus of crony capitalism engulfed the realm of natural resources, from spectrum to coal, where the government insisted on parcelling out resources on a discretionary basis. It spilled over to the infrastructure sector where public–private partnerships were absolutely necessary to cover the gaping holes that constituted the very foundations of the economy, but where contracts that seemed to privatise profit and socialise losses, took away the sheen from an important exercise. By 2012, the public perception was of a scam where there was a direct interface between unscrupulous entrepreneurs and corrupt government officials. The legitimacy of the entire post-1991 order was under question. The system seemed rotten, unfair and irreparable. A populist backlash was inevitable and was symbolised by popular movements against corruption. The danger of such populism was that it risked throwing the baby out with the bathwater. India needed to be rid of crony capitalism, but not capitalism. More government, and bigger government would have taken us back to the pre-1991 era from which the country had emerged in fortuitous circumstances yielding real gains in terms of higher growth and unprecedented poverty alleviation.

The arrival of the then Gujarat Chief Minister Narendra Modi on the national stage as the BJP's prime ministerial candidate in 2013 was a much-needed antidote to the populist backlash. Modi campaigned on his track record as the long-serving chief minister of Gujarat; the state had grown at 'China-esque' rates under his leadership.

Significantly, it was a live example of an enabling State and thriving entrepreneurship within the overall policy framework of the Government of India. Clearly, India's overarching policy architecture provided possibilities for growth and for transformation. Interestingly, Modi was perhaps the first mainstream politician in India who campaigned on the promise of 'Minimum Government, Maximum Governance'. There was considerable misinterpretation of what this meant. Modi was never going to be a Ronald Reagan or Margaret Thatcher presiding over a withdrawal of the State from the economic sphere. At India's level of per capita income, the State still has an important role to play and there is no mass political constituency for free market economics of the Thatcher–Reagan variety. The US and UK were already advanced economies when the free market revolution happened. Even in East Asia, the State played an important role in enabling transformation. However, it is important to get the role of the State right—it must be a facilitator and regulator, not a controller—and to recognise the importance of the private sector sans crony capitalists in India's future transformation. That is what Prime Minister Modi promised to set right as he took office.

This book is a collection of articles that presents arguments on why India needs to place greater faith in free market forces if it is to achieve a transformation and why Prime Minister Modi has, over the last four years, laid the foundation for a transformation by right-sizing and reorienting government, fighting cronyism, encouraging honest entrepreneurship and putting the onus of transforming India on not just the government and private sector, but on every individual Indian.

MODI

INTRODUCTION: MODI

It is a hard task to tame the leviathan Government of India. It is to Prime Minister Narendra Modi's credit that he confronted the reality of a quite dysfunctional State head on. For long, and quite persistently, India's government had played a counter-productive role in India's economic story doing too much of what it should not be doing at all (dabbling in business and the business of business) and too little of what it should have focused on (physical and social infrastructure). After liberalisation in 1991, the State beat a retreat from some spheres of the economy thus becoming less counter-productive. However, the State never reformed itself to play the productive role of an enabler for the economy. Since assuming office in 2014, Modi has reimagined and rejigged the scope, ambition and performance of the government. In doing so, he has laid the foundation for a sustained and inclusive growth led by the private sector with the government acting as facilitator.

The first corrective step taken by Modi is to get the government to do less of what it should not do. The determined effort to cut red tape and improve India's Ease of Doing Business rankings from the 140s to 100 in the World Bank survey is an excellent example of that approach. Modi's government has also restarted the strategic disinvestment programme after a gap of more than a decade to get the business out of the business of business. Among the thirty-four public sector companies approved for strategic disinvestment by the Cabinet is Air India, a chronic loss-maker, symbolic of why the government is unable to run businesses.

The second corrective step is about a new focus on improving the efficiency with which the government does what it ought to—implement programmes and projects as critical enablers for the economy, namely physical infrastructure and social sectors like health, education, nutrition and sanitation. For this, the government has worked to switching its expenditure away from populist consumption expenditure—subsidies and doles—to productive investment expenditure while maintaining fiscal discipline. It has also established systems to monitor the implementation of its plans. The prime minister personally monitors and troubleshoots key infrastructure projects through his regular interaction via video conference with all Secretaries of the Government of India, Chief Secretaries of twenty-nine states and administrators of all Union Territories. There is also a careful monitoring of outcomes (not just outputs) and ministries are held accountable for the money they spend or indeed do not spend. In areas where the problem isn't just the quantum of spending but finding new systems of delivery to replace broken ones, there is a creativity in approach. In health for example, the government has conceived the use of a market instrument—namely insurance—to provide health care coverage to the poor who have been let down by the dysfunctional system of government hospitals.

The third step in redefining government has been to devolve power (and finances) away from New Delhi. It took almost seventy years for a prime minister to take the bold step of abolishing centralised planning, five year plans and the Planning

Commission which usually advocated one-size-fits-all policies for a very diverse—not just culturally, but also economically—country. Modi has given federalism the teeth it deserves. Indeed, it is critical that states play their part as defined in the Constitution in the governance and development of India. In several areas where the next generation of reforms is required, whether agriculture, land or labour, states have to play a leading role. It is only when Team India, comprising the Union Government, state governments and local governments, works in a constructive combination of cooperation and competition that India will transform. The chapters in this section present arguments on how Modi's tenure has laid the foundations for a new India.

THE REAL IMPORTANCE OF MODI'S RISE: A CM AS PM

This article was first published in January 2014, four months after Narendra Modi was named as prime ministerial candidate by the BJP, and four months before he became prime minister. It was the first time that an Indian chief minister was campaigning for prime minister based on his record of governance as chief minister. That was a transformative moment in Indian politics.

The rise and rise of Narendra Modi is the big political story—since he was named the BJP's prime ministerial candidate in September 2013. The results of the CNN IBN-CSDS* Election Tracker were revealing. In July 2013, nineteen per cent of respondents said that Modi was their preferred choice for prime minister. Six months later, in January 2014, that number shot up to thirty-four per cent. Modi's anointment as his party's prime ministerial candidate lifted the BJP's fortunes.

Modi's rise is interesting for several reasons. But none is perhaps more important than the fact that he has broken the glass ceiling for regional leaders in the insular Delhi-based

* A survey carried out by one of the foremost English TV news channels in the country, along with the Centre for the Study of Developing Societies.

national leaderships of major parties. The Congress has always kept its High Command, presided over by the Gandhi family, at an elevated level. If a non-Gandhi has become prime minister or prime minister candidate, it is at the pleasure of the High Command. State chief ministers are permanently on a lower pedestal and any explicit or implicit aspiration for a shot at the top job could result in their fall from even that lower rung.

But the BJP has been no different—for the purposes of Lok Sabha elections—with the Delhi-based 'national' leadership—whether Atal Bihari Vajpayee or L.K. Advani—traditionally holding the balance of power. Modi has broken through. He has shown that it is indeed possible to project success at the regional level on to the bigger national stage. That he comes from a mid-size state, which sends only twenty-six MPs to the Lok Sabha—and which isn't in the politically dominant Hindi heartland—makes his foray into the 'national' psyche even more impressive.

Of course, Modi is not the first person who served as chief minister to be a prime ministerial candidate—Morarji Desai and V.P. Singh would claim that mantle though they became prime ministers much after their tenures as chief ministers had finished. Modi wasn't the first serving chief minister to become prime minister—that place in history is taken by H.D. Deve Gowda. But unlike Desai, and Singh (who were national Delhi-based leaders rather than regional satraps when they became prime minister) and the accidental Gowda, Modi was the first chief minister who was running for the country's top job on the plank of his track record (of good governance) as a successful chief minister.

This is an encouraging trend for India from a governance point of view. The real nuts and bolts of governance are best learnt at the state level. It is state governments which ultimately deliver most public services—whether education, health, roads and power—and welfare programmes. It is in the efficient delivery of these services and programmes that India faces its most daunting challenges. 'National' leaders who have never served in the states are unlikely to be as well versed with the nuts and bolts of policy implementation that state leaders are. That has been one of the fatal flaws of the Congress-led UPA, which has missed the wisdom and experience of successful regional leaders in government.

The ascendancy of a serving chief minister to the country's top job also provided a much needed boost to federalism. There is only so much the Central Government in Delhi can do to deliver all that India needs. In fact, there are several contentious policy spaces like labour laws which are best left to the states, rather than to a coalition-constrained Centre. Modi knows that. He is in a good place to devolve more power to states, particularly on the nitty-gritty of implementation while the Centre only sets the broad policy agenda.

Needless to say, Modi is not forever. But the demonstration effect of his rise has prompted other regional stalwarts (from the BJP and from non-BJP, non-Congress parties) to go national in the years to come. Of course, there is no guarantee of success. Some regional stalwarts have tried and failed in their national ambition. Both Mulayam Singh Yadav and Mayawati have tried to step out of Uttar Pradesh, but it is their less than stellar track records in governance rather than their regional confine that have proved a stumbling block.

The Modi Model is a delicious prospect for India's democracy, federalism and governance. That will remain Modi's real legacy.

(This article was first published in *Firstpost.com*)

THE MODI PARADIGM

This article was first published in May 2017 when the Modi government completed three years in office. The paradigm defined here continues to elucidate the guiding framework of the government.

In May 2017, Prime Minister Narendra Modi's government completes three years in office. There will, no doubt, be a flurry of report cards from experts and from the media. Most of them will focus on the nitty-gritty of what has or has not been accomplished. Not many will paint the big picture. However, the larger canvas or the underlying philosophy of governance matters, because all the nitty-gritty flows from it. The fact is that Modi's economic policies are based on a radically different paradigm than that of previous governments.

The new canvas is brushed with two broad strokes: a new federalism (cooperative and competitive) and minimum government, maximum governance. Put together, the unambiguous messages are as follows. First, New Delhi alone cannot transform India—it needs a partnership of the Union and states, a point the prime minister reiterated by invoking the spirit of Team India at the third meeting of the Governing Council of the NITI Aayog on 23 April 2017.

Second, the government will have to do things very differently (less activity in some spheres, much more activity in others) if India is to advance rapidly, a point that the prime minister made at the Civil Services Day on 2 April 2017 when he exhorted bureaucrats to be enablers rather than regulators.

Minimum Government

This paradigm shift doesn't lend itself to the kind of easy categorisation of 'Right' or 'Left' economists and commentators are used to. Minimum government, when understood as the kind practised by Margaret Thatcher in the UK or Ronald Reagan in the US, meant a complete retreat of the State from spheres of economic activity. Narendra Modi's version means that the State retreats from spheres where it plays an obviously counterproductive role, like in making it difficult to do business through over-regulation (there is a commitment to improve India's ranking in the World Bank's Ease of Doing Business survey from 130 to fifty) or by overspending and busting the fiscal deficit, particularly on careless populism, with the end results being a crowding out of the productive private sector—which could use the same resources more efficiently—and the unleashing of inflationary pressures on the economy.

On the public sector, there is an attempt to weed out the underperforming enterprises which cannot survive without government dole while strengthening and giving autonomy to those which can thrive.

But it's important to remember that minimum government is suffixed by maximum governance. At India's level of per capita income, the State cannot retreat altogether. However, it has to be more efficient in carrying out its activities, whether it is the essential task of providing security/law and order or the provision of public goods like sanitation, primary education and primary health care, or in the building of critical infrastructure like roads, ports and railways, all areas where private sector participation is bound to be limited.

The government must also, in a targeted and sustainable way, invest in the poorest—this it has done through schemes like subsidised (but not free) insurance (life, accident and crop failure) and the Ujjwala Yojana for giving LPG connections to the poorest households. The entire emphasis on maximum governance is to ensure that more transparent and accountable methods are found to effectively deliver these goods, services and interventions. Hence the emphasis on Aadhaar and direct benefits transfer on the one hand, and transparent auctions and bidding for large projects on the other.

Cooperative Federalism

Ultimately, for India as a whole, the force multiplier for maximum governance will come from embracing cooperative and competitive federalism. The long history of Independent India has mostly been about an unequal relationship between the 'Centre' (the correct constitutional reference is Union) and the states. The centralised planning paradigm cemented the idea of New Delhi controlling the development trajectory of every state. A one-size-fits-all approach was deemed to be the best way forward despite obvious differences between states.

Narendra Modi's long experience as chief minister (unusual for an Indian prime minister) gave him a different lens. The abolition of the Planning Commission, rationalisation of centrally-sponsored schemes and greater devolution of finances to the states by the 14th Finance Commission laid the platform for the new paradigm. For the first time, states have a say in Union policy—subcommittees of chief ministers have studied Skill India, Swachh Bharat, centrally sponsored schemes and digital payments. The implementation of the Goods and Services Tax (GST) is another excellent example of cooperative federalism. Also, for the first time, New Delhi is not creating or forcing down giant spending schemes where the states must implement the Union's diktat.

The complement to cooperative federalism is competitive federalism. Competition should not and cannot be about a race to the bottom. What is envisaged is a race to the top as states compete with one another on various parameters, some explicitly measured, some not.

Constitutionally, several critical policy subjects are in the domain of states (either in the state list or concurrent list) including land and labour policies, education and health. On land and labour, which are in the concurrent list, the Union government is encouraging states to legislate liberal laws. Some states have begun working on these.

The NITI Aayog is facilitating the work on land through providing model land-leasing laws. There is now a ranking of states on the Ease of Doing Business. There will soon be indices for health, education and water outcomes. New Delhi's role is limited to conceptualising the indices and monitoring their integrity and, of course, sharing best practices and model laws. The rest is in the domain of states. A demanding electorate across India will hold state leaders accountable for their performance just as they hold to account the Union government's performance. Eventually, the transformation of India requires a transformation in each of its twenty-nine states. It cannot be achieved without a partnership between New Delhi and each of the state capitals.

This philosophy of governance is radically different from the previous 'Centre at the centre' and 'maximum government' approach. Rarely do transformations happen overnight, but in the right environment they can happen reasonably quickly. Critics will quibble about the nitty-gritty, but the big picture is this: Modi has provided a unique opening for transformation.

(This article was first published in *The Hindu*.)

FOR MORAL CAPITALISM

This article was first published in October 2017. With his personal integrity intact, Narendra Modi remains the politician most likely to make a convincing case for a cronyism-free capitalism in India.

India's politics is uncomfortable with the idea of wealth creation. India's politicians are immersed in wealth creation. That is the cruel paradox at the heart of Independent India's inability to climb to a double-digit growth trajectory. For, if any nation wishes to become prosperous in quick time, it must grow at a furious pace by continuously creating vast sums of wealth. Indian politics has stifled that ambition. Indian politicians have nearly killed it. The path to prosperity is hardly a secret; many nations in the West and East have achieved it over the last two centuries. But every country needs an enabling environment for it to happen. For most of India's history since 1947, the political economy has provided a poor substratum. Prime Minister Modi has taken some steps to shift the ground, but it will take perseverance and reform before a long counter-productive legacy is folded away.

Being the dominant party at the time of Independence, the Congress laid down the principles which would drive India's economy, polity and society. Neither Gandhi nor Jawaharlal

Nehru, despite the considerable divergence of their views on the economy, gave primacy to the notion of private wealth creation. While Gandhi was very focused on small-scale industry and a self-sufficient rural economy, Nehru's economic vision was influenced by the (erstwhile) Soviet Union in which the State and enterprises owned by it would be at the commanding heights of the economy. After two centuries of Colonialism, one of which involved direct rule by the East India Company, a private capitalist enterprise, there was a general suspicion of the profit motive. B.R. Ambedkar may have temporarily prevailed by preventing the insertion of the word 'Socialist' in the Constitution—he did not believe that the founders of the Republic should tie India down to one system forever—but it was the Left-wing of the Congress which dominated India for the first four decades after Independence. For the dominant Congress, poverty alleviation was the main slogan. Somehow, wealth creation was not a strategy adopted for that noble end goal. That has continued till this day, when Nehru's great-grandson is in effect the leader of the party.

The BJP has had less influence on the political economy of Independent India, having ruled at the Centre just once in a coalition (between 1998 and 2004) before Modi won a parliamentary majority in 2014. But now that it is the major national party, its thinking matters. The Integral Humanism of Deendayal Upadhyaya, the long serving chief of the Jana Sangh in post-1947 India, is the philosophical foundation of the BJP's economic thinking. Upadhyaya was critical of both socialism and capitalism, which he believed were too focused on materialism (artha and kama) while neglecting dharma and moksha, not defined as religiosity *per se* but as a set of values and a spirituality beyond the material. The BJP's intellectual mooring does not entirely reject wealth creation even if it does not put it upfront. And the traditional core constituency of the BJP has consisted of wealth creators.

Of course, India's economy and indeed the global economy have evolved over time. The most damage inflicted upon the economy was when Indira Gandhi became prime minister and policies took a sharp turn Left-ward. The Congress aversion to private profit only became stronger and resulted in the nationalisation of banks, restriction of foreign investment and draconian laws restricting the size of enterprises. In 1947, India may have needed the government to play a big role. By the 1960s, the task of wealth generation should have shifted to the private sector, which had greater capacity, as it did in many East Asian countries. However, India's political economy went in a different direction. The word 'Socialist' was inserted into the Constitution.

India's boom years ought to have created a constituency of young Indians who'd have greater faith in wealth creation and free markets than earlier generations did.

A pernicious side effect of the shift was the introduction of a licence-quota raj which allowed some selected private entrepreneurs to flourish at the expense of efficiency and consumer interest while forming a close nexus with government. It was the years between 1966 and 1977 that saw a culture of corruption take deep roots. India had to deal with a double whammy. Ostensibly, wealth creation and private profit were discouraged, leading to low rates of growth. However, the fostering of a small crony capitalist elite meant that capitalism would acquire a bad name. Capitalism thrives only when there are competitive free markets and not when the government controls them tightly. But socialist India knew only two kinds of capitalism—the East India Company kind and the crony kind.

A decisive break from socialism took place in 1991 in the backdrop of an economic crisis. The existence of a crisis provided politics a cover for undertaking radical reforms which disturbed vested interests. The dreaded licence-quota raj was quickly dismantled for a number of industries and sectors. For the first time, private enterprise, whether domestic or foreign had the freedom to grow wings. Unfortunately, politics never changed its rhetoric. P.V. Narasimha Rao, India's reformist prime minister, could never quite summon himself to do a Deng Xiaoping by declaring that 'to be rich is glorious.' He couldn't even make the other famous Deng proclamation, 'It doesn't matter if the cat is black or white, as long as it catches mice.' Politics would continue to reform by stealth while pretending to be socialist in public.

Things may have finally changed in the first decade of the 2000s when the government of Atal Bihari Vajpayee went ahead with several bold reforms, including the privatisation of some public sector companies. This was also the period when Indian IT, led by the likes of Infosys, Wipro and HCL became world beaters without any help from the government. No one grudged the wealth India's IT entrepreneurs generated because it was seen as justly earned. Unfortunately, the defeat of India's first non-socialist government in 2004 turned the clock back. Ironically enough, the period between 2003 and 2012, which saw India's highest ever growth of nine per cent plus per annum, laid the seeds for a further de-legitimisation of capitalism, capitalists, politics, politicians and the wealth they had accumulated.

India's boom years ought to have created a constituency of young Indians, who grew up in liberalised India, who would have a much greater faith in wealth creation and free markets than earlier generations did. However, the virulent crony capitalism that was unleashed in the boom years ended in policy paralysis and slowdown post 2012. The problem wasn't free markets but continued government discretion in sectors like telecom, coal and other natural resources. Public–private partnerships which were mooted to solve India's infrastructure deficit descended into a farce, with profits privatised and losses socialised. So even while a majority of Indians benefitted from high growth, the perception that too many people had acquired wealth based on a nexus with government stood out. The rich and wealthy were deemed crooked, just like the East India Company or the entrepreneurs of the 1970s. That many politicians became businessmen and *crorepatis* many times over in the post-liberalisation era also turned public perception against the manner in which the system had evolved. The scale of corruption and wealth accumulation by sundry politicians took on a whole new dimension compared with the pre-1991 era.

The challenge for India and India's current leader is to separate genuine wealth creation from crony capitalism. Prime Minister Modi is trying hard. He has taken strict action against corruption and cronyism, while encouraging genuine entrepreneurship, particularly in the young generation through initiatives like Startup India. He is the first Indian leader to openly campaign on the promise of minimum government in a country where the government has been larger than life even after 1991. Modi's personal integrity is a great asset in his quest to convince India of the merits of honest wealth creation. Unlike many other politicians, he is not using politics as an avenue to enrich himself or his family. That gives him an unusual legitimacy and moral authority. The fact is that India cannot solve the problem of poverty or complete its quest for inclusiveness by redistributing a small cake. The size of the cake needs urgent expansion and only wealth creation can do that.

Modi has an intellectual anchor in his quest. Deendayal Upadhyaya's philosophy of Integral Humanism could play an important role in creating a framework for a well-functioning market economy which eschews cronyism and other types of wrongdoing while creating wealth. Integral Humanism has a moral dimension which is important in a country reeling from amoral, if not immoral, capitalists.

Perhaps, unlike Deng Xiaoping, we should care about the colour of the cat.

(This article was first published in the *Open* magazine.)

MODI, RAHUL AND THE FIGHT FOR INDIA'S PROSPERITY

This article was first published in May 2015. Three years on, as the country readies for the next general election in 2019, voters will have to choose between the two different economic visions for India described in this piece.

If he is to persuade India, Narendra Modi needs to be radical in policy reform and sprightly in execution.

Everyone loves a political dogfight. So, it is no surprise that Rahul Gandhi's holding-no-punches comeback to frontline politics has attracted much attention. A constant battle between Prime Minister Narendra Modi and the presumptive leader of the leading Opposition party will quite obviously be a feature of politics, at least until 2019. But what is more important than the clash of two contrasting personalities is the battle of ideas that could define where India ends up two decades from now. India's raucous political economy is nowhere near a consensus on the policy path ahead.

It would be easy to conclude that Modi has the better grasp of what India wants. After all, he won the first single party majority in three decades just a year ago, something many political scientists thought a fractured Indian polity had abandoned for good. But the reality is that the mandate was probably more a vote against corruption and inflation, the two evils promoted by the Congress-led United Progressive Alliance government, than a conclusive vote for a more positive agenda. Narendra Modi's vision is clear. For prosperity, he believes India needs to industrialise—that's what 'Make in India' is about. That is the only way to draw people out of agriculture and make that sector more productive. To better the lives of Indians, he knows India needs to urbanise in a more orderly fashion than before—that is what the 100 'smart cities' are about. He knows that prosperity requires the generation of wealth by the private sector—that is why he has committed to building infrastructure and easing the constraints of doing business. He also knows the poor can't be left behind, but instead of wasteful subsidies and doles, he wants to include them in the mainstream through innovative schemes like the Jan Dhan Yojana, the Rashtriya Swasthya Bima Yojana and through direct cash transfers.

Narendra Modi's is a textbook vision. No country has become rich without developing a manufacturing base and without shrinking the workforce involved in agriculture; without vibrant cities and without a majority of the population living in them; and without a wealth-generating private sector. Modi should have the argument wrapped up, but he doesn't. A major part of his problem is that people are not seeing the conversion of that vision into reality quickly enough; another is that his government hasn't created the right policy frameworks for that vision to be executed. India's laws and regulations remain more suited to an old-fashioned socialist economy than a modern market economy. If he is to persuade India, Modi needs to be radical in policy reform and sprightly in execution; he needs to show change in the next four years.

Meanwhile, Rahul Gandhi is going to try and tell India that Narendra Modi is on the wrong track. At the centre of his argument is the fact that Modi's strategy will do little for India's poor and only favour the rich. That argument will always have some appeal in a country where some 300 million people still live in absolute poverty. However, if Rahul Gandhi thinks he can win the argument by promising a rural idyll, where fifty per cent of India's workforce will continue to plough farms producing less than fifteen per cent of GDP, he is wrong. He needs to define a plan for prosperity because India's poor don't want to remain mired in poverty. They aren't reflexively against wealth creators either, as long as they see that those wealth creators are also generating jobs for the average Indian. Sure, Rahul should rail against crony capitalism but not miss the wood for the trees. India needs a vibrant, competitive private sector to generate jobs. Rahul Gandhi must have a vision of his own to show how this can be done, which could be different from Modi's. It could involve greater State intervention, better regulation and a more transparent government. But he will have to be particularly persuasive to sell his party to India given its horrendous recent record in government.

Of course, if Modi fails to deliver his vision of India, Rahul Gandhi may find a way back by default. But that won't serve India's interests. With a limited pro-poverty rather than pro-poor agenda, Rahul Gandhi can never be a change agent. If ever he comes to power on that kind of agenda, failure is guaranteed, just like it was for UPA-II.

Any process of reform and churning—and India will continuously go through both in one way or another in the next decade and longer—creates winners and losers. The best politicians deftly manage both sides. With Narendra Modi, there is a risk (at least of perception) that he will side disproportionately with the winners. With Rahul Gandhi, there is a risk that he will undermine the winners and empathise (via paltry doles) with the losers. Neither is a sustainable political economy. Both scenarios will lead to a backlash from one group or another. Whichever man finds the better balance and efficient execution will govern India for the longer time. He will also convert India from a poor nation to a rich one.

(This article was first published in *The Hindu*.)

MODINOMICS SHOULD FOCUS ON TRUST, NOT TRUSTEESHIP

This article was first published in March 2014, two months before Modi's victory in the 2014 general elections. It is a critique of Modi's argument in favour of trusteeship à la Gandhi and an argument in favour of building trust instead. To a great extent, Modi has succeeded in restoring the trust of the people of India in the government which was badly broken after the corruption-ridden years of the UPA.

Prime Minister Narendra Modi has said that the core of his economic thinking can be captured by one word—trusteeship, a principle propounded by Mahatma Gandhi, which in Modi's view very simply means that the government should not behave like the owner of the country's resources but instead as a trustee of the people (the real owners). In contrast to the UPA's crony capitalist style plundering natural resources, trusteeship seems like a fine idea.

In practical terms, it may be a non-starter. The real problem with trusteeship is that it frowns on private profit. And it is unrealistic (and inefficient) not to promote private profit, even in natural resources. Therefore, Modi should make 'trust'—another word he has mentioned several times—rather than trusteeship the core of his policy thinking.

What's the simplest way for the government to be a 'non-exploitative' (since ownership presumably has a connotation of exploitation) trustee of the country's resources? It can let resources lie idle. Let coal and iron ore be underground; let airwaves be unutilised, etc. But if a resource is not exploited at all, it is of no benefit to the people on whose behalf the government is acting as a trustee.

What's the next best way? For the government to try and exploit the resources on its own via public sector entities (on the peoples' behalf of course)? At least that way no natural resources can be used for private profit. All the profits would accrue to the people of India, the real owners of PSUs.

Unfortunately, the people of India know to their detriment how awry such an approach can go. Just look at Coal India, the monopoly producer and seller in the open market of coal. It makes a lot of profit which goes to the people of India via the exchequer. But it has no incentive to produce the amount of coal necessary for India's huge power requirements. Can anyone imagine what would be the state of India's telecom sector if the right to use airwaves had been given only to BSNL and MTNL? We wouldn't have the private sector making profit of a natural resource, but we would have paid a heavy price in the form of high tariffs and had limited connectivity.

The UPA government did the country (and itself) a great disservice in the dubious allocation of 2G spectrum and the allocation of captive coal blocks. But it would be unwise for another government to throw out capitalism with the cronies. Telecom is the best example of how the government can give up the ownership/trusteeship of a natural resource (spectrum) and how capitalists can own the resource and make private profit while bringing huge benefits to the people of India.

The point, of course, is that the people of India must be able to 'trust' their government to allocate natural resources for commercial exploitation in a proper, fair and transparent fashion. The UPA has destroyed that trust. Modi needs to earn it back.

Natural resources are exploited for private profit everywhere in the world. India can be no different. Of course, there is a need for regulation to ensure that all players are playing by the rules of the game. But to do away with private profit in the exploitation of natural resources is to take India back to the 1950s. It is expecting too much from capitalists, as Gandhi did, to act as trustees and not use their profits for personal gains. Capitalists are simply not going to invest their profit in society, except that if they do an efficient and honest job of exploiting the resources, the country and its people will benefit—from better mobile connectivity, faster internet, more power, cheaper power etc.

The people of India also need to trust corporates that their businesses are run transparently, with no hanky-panky. India Inc. hasn't always set the highest standards. Perhaps Modi can persuade India Inc. to mend its ways in exchange for opportunities to continue to make profit of natural resources. That kind of trust building is also necessary,

Of course, the government and the private sector need to start trusting each other (rather than bribing each other) after an awful five years under UPA-II. That is the only way to end crony capitalism and to weed out the bad eggs.

It is the trust deficits between the people and government, India Inc. and government, and the people and India Inc. which need to be bridged before India can return to a higher trajectory of growth.

To become the trustee of the nation's resources, Modi first needs to win the trust of a majority. If he does, he should make trust, not trusteeship, the central word of his economic philosophy.

(This article was first published in *Firstpost.com*)

DEMONETISATION IS FOR THE LONG RUN

This article was first published in December 2016, one month after Prime Minister Modi announced his decision to withdraw high value currency notes from circulation. Much commentary has appeared on the short run impact of demonetisation. But, as argued in this piece, the real positive impact of demonetisation can only be gauged over the long run.

The critics of demonetisation are absolutely right about the adverse short-term impact of the policy. It has caused major inconvenience to a vast majority, particularly to those who have the least financial resources. Of course, it will shave off some amount of GDP growth for anywhere between a quarter and three quarters because of the economic disruption it has caused in different sectors of the economy. According to some, including the venerable Dr Manmohan Singh, this alone is sufficient to damn demonetisation. After all, the short run is all that matters because in the long run, as Keynes famously said, we are all dead.

While that proposition may be true for individuals, it certainly isn't true for nations. India has a long-term future even if you and I don't. Also, there is a medium term, longer than an electoral cycle or two (certainly longer than a quarter or two) but shorter than a generation (say, thirty years). The real impact of demonetisation must be weighed in the medium/long term.

India's economic progress is at an inflexion point. Twenty-five years of liberalisation have yielded far superior outcomes for almost every Indian than four and a half decades of socialism did. But the gradual opening of markets with continued, substantial government control over the economy also unleashed a virulent strain of crony (and indeed phoney) capitalism at about the same time that India grew at its fastest between 2003 and 2012. Rules and fairness were simply cast aside. The policy paralysis in UPA-II and the spectacular downfall of a government that had won an unprecedented second consecutive full term in office (a first post-1991) was a backlash against cronyism and loot.

It is to Narendra Modi's credit that he was able to separate the virtues of capitalism from the pitfalls of crony capitalism in his campaign for India's highest office. Thus the rhetoric of minimum government (pro-market) went hand in hand with the rhetoric against black money and illicit wealth accumulation (anti-crony). But the sustainability of pro-market policies is only feasible if there is a firm stamping out of cronyism. Otherwise, it is easy for public perception to view any pro-market policy as pro-business and pro-crony. Eventually, if that perception makes strong roots, India's relative economic success over the last quarter century could be quickly eroded by a populist backlash.

It is, therefore, important to put demonetisation in the context of this political economy. The reason that opinion polls and anecdotal evidence continue to suggest the popularity of the move despite the obvious hardships is because it is perceived as a decisive act against the crooked—those who made their money unscrupulously and then chose to hide it—not the rich/well-off who earned legitimately and paid their taxes.

Technology-enabled Transparency

This is no throwback to Indira Gandhi-style socialist populism. For a start, it is not confiscatory—your money remains yours provided you are willing to disclose it. More importantly, Prime Minister Modi remains committed to markets and entrepreneurship of the rules-based variety. That commitment is evident in other policy measures being implemented. The removal of discretion in the auctioning of all natural resources has already happened. There is a move to technology-enabled transparency elsewhere in government. Unsurprisingly, there has been no corruption scandal even as the government completes half its tenure. There is a new emphasis on the 'personal' sector (moving away from a singular obsession with public sector or private sector jobs to productive self-employment), through schemes like Startup India and Stand-up India and through a commitment to get the government out of the business of doing business.

But the success of all of that depends on rooting out the hold of crony capitalists in the system. Demonetisation is an important step in dislocating those who don't play by the rules of the game.

It is often asked why politicians have failed to make a case for the free market in India. At least part of the answer lies in the widespread cronyism which gives the free market a bad name. If any politician is ever to make that case—and for now Modi seems the likeliest to do so—he or she has to eliminate crony capitalism.

A system will be viewed as fair if no individual or business is able to manipulate the rules of the game whether in terms of gaining favours from the government or by evading taxes. Free markets and capitalism will get mass public support if everyone is on a level playing field and when the rich/well off pay their taxes which can then be used to invest in those left behind so that they too have an opportunity to rise.

It is only a rule-based capitalism—sans cronies and phonies—combined with a clean government that can transform India. It is said that the quality of India's democracy is what gives it an edge over authoritarian China. That will hold true if democracy delivers a rules-based capitalism and efficient government. It is a tortuous path but few nations in history have got there easily.

That is why a long-term view is important. It is easy to be cynical and say that demonetisation will not alter the behaviour of the crooked. It may not change everyone but it will nudge a certain number in the right direction—to pay taxes, to transact without cash. More importantly, demonetisation will rebuild the faith of a disenchanted people in staying invested in a system that is rotten but that can still become fairer for all. The crooks don't have the keys to power and influence in perpetuity. That's an important message as India aspires to prosperity for all.

(This article was first published in *The Hindu*.)

CENTRIST MODI SURPRISES HIS CRITICS

This article was first published in December 2014. The 'liberal' clamour on rising intolerance under Modi's regime has only grown louder since then. However, the Prime Minister has studiously stuck to the centre ground, chiding the extremist statements made by individuals associated with the ruling party or its affiliates.

Has India become more intolerant since Narendra Modi became prime minister? Modi's critics on the liberal Left—and there are many—certainly think so and they blame the prime minister for it. Modi's critics, still reeling from his stunning general election win—and subsequent electoral successes in Maharashtra, Haryana, Jharkhand and Jammu and Kashmir—will happily clutch at straws in an attempt to corner him. Indeed, it is their right to do so.

The fact is that Narendra Modi has stuck studiously to the political Centre. It's interesting how the liberal commentariat has chosen to ignore Modi's frequent visits—almost one every month since he took office—to Jammu and Kashmir, India's only Muslim-majority state. He spent the Hindu festival of Diwali with the largely Muslim people of the Kashmir Valley, in solidarity with their suffering after massive floods. Modi, the 'Hindu nationalist' chose to address an election rally in Srinagar, something few mainstream national politicians do, a brave and inclusive gesture.

Instead, critics have chosen to focus on one stray utterance of Sadhvi Niranjan Jyoti, one admittedly unnecessary comment made by Sushma Swaraj, and one instance of *ghar-vapsi* somewhere near Agra. Needless to say, Modi is not responsible for any of this. He condemned the Sadhvi's statement. He has been relentless in saying that the Indian State has only one holy book: the Constitution. And he has privately disapproved of mass *ghar-vapsi* programmes—the BJP is not backing them and has said so in parliament.

Consider the most contentious issue of conversions and why it is the wrong stick to beat Modi with. In principle, there is nothing illegal or unconstitutional about re-conversions to Hinduism, just as there is no restriction on conversions to Christianity and Islam.

Just how many Left-liberals have raised their voice against the conversion practices—often involving coercion and inducement—of Christian missionaries? How many raised their voice when the former Andhra Pradesh Chief Minister Y.S. Rajasekhar Reddy, a 'secular' Congressman, gave tacit state support to Christian missionaries? To be consistent, liberals either need to be equally agitated about all conversions, or be totally unconcerned about them. Targetting *ghar-vapsi* alone is hypocritical.

Modi's insistence on sticking to the political Centre is a risky strategy for him. It threatens to alienate two crucial support bases—the cultural Right in the wider Sangh Parivar, and the economic Right, which is banking on him to unleash radical free-market reforms. What makes Modi a particularly talented politician is precisely this ability to take risks and defy the conventional wisdom. He isn't going to follow any textbook politics or economics. His critics, on the other hand, very much stick to the textbook. Remember how Modi was accused of communalising the campaign for the general election, when in reality the Congress and some regional parties like the Samajwadi Party had a greater stake in fanning the flames of communal tension? Modi's critics targeted him and let the others off the hook. The people of India gave Modi the benefit of doubt.

It needs a politician of extreme dexterity and ability to govern India well. His critics are jumping the gun and attributing to him fringe extremism that he is not responsible for and does not approve of.

(This article was first published in *The Sunday Guardian*.)

MODINOMICS IS NOT THATCHERITE: IT IS A MIX OF DENG AND LEE

This article was first published in May 2014, just days before Modi was sworn in as Prime Minister of India. The economic policies of Modi's government in its first four years have drawn criticism from those who believed his philosophy would be similar to Ronald Reagan and Margaret Thatcher. However, it was wrong to even assume that Modi was ever a free marketer in the Anglo-Saxon mould. In fact, his economic policies have mirrored those of East Asian economies as this article had predicted.

Is Prime Minister Narendra Modi India's answer to Margaret Thatcher and Ronald Reagan, the radically pro-free market leaders of the UK and US from the 1980s? For those tired and despondent about the counter-productive role played by the Indian State—whether entrepreneurs, managers, economists or even ordinary citizens—India needs a Reagan–Thatcher moment. However, Modi is unlikely to emulate either Thatcher or Reagan in any hurry. The more apt global comparisons for Modi are Deng Xiaoping and Lee Kuan Yew and NOT because he intends to be authoritarian like them.

The most salient features of the economics that defined the legacy of Thatcher and Reagan were:

1. Aggressive privatisation of state-owned entities

2. Deep deregulation of the financial sector
3. A long period of tight monetary policy
4. A crushing of labour unions

Modi isn't likely to pursue any of these objectives in the short term. He has repeatedly said that he sees value in public sector enterprises and would prefer to grant them autonomy than privatise.

He isn't an outspoken advocate of aggressive financial sector liberalisation much like the economist Jagdish Bhagwati (who has openly advised Modi) who favours liberalisation of trade and industry more than financial sector liberalisation.

Modi's party, the BJP (led by his close confidant, Arun Jaitley), has insisted for several months that interest rates must come down, not go up despite almost chronic inflation. Modi and his team (rightly) believe that inflation is a result of supply side bottlenecks and not excess demand.

On the fourth issue, of labour, Modi is unlikely to dismantle India's labour laws in a hurry and risk confrontation with unions. He may instead adopt the more pragmatic approach of letting states decide on labour laws rather than the Centre. Overall, on available evidence, Modi isn't a Thatcherite barring his no-nonsense attitude to politics and government. He isn't even remotely Reagan, the one-time actor and sunny Californian who was hardly tough by personality.

So does that mean all hope for free markets and radical reform is wishful thinking? No. It's just that Modi's role models are likely to be found closer to home, in East Asia, as a matter of fact in China and Singapore (and perhaps Japan), countries which were at India's level of development when they began to reform rather than the US and UK which were already advanced economies when Reagan and Thatcher took over. What were the salient features of Deng Xiaoping's reformist economics (and to a large extent Lee Kuan Yew's as well) which transformed China (and Singapore)?

1. An open policy for Foreign Direct Investment
2. An easy business environment for private enterprises
3. Heavy State investment in infrastructure, both physical (roads, ports etc) and social (education, health) but limited doles
4. An important (but autonomous) role for public sector enterprises
5. Low interest rates to buoy investment
6. In China's case, a strong emphasis on devolution of powers to provinces

There is every likelihood that Modi's government will adopt each of these as guiding principles of its policies. The government of Gujarat adopted the first four principles when Modi was chief minister. Points five and six need the Central Government to implement.

Of course, it was easier for both Deng and Lee to implement their policies in what were essentially one-party authoritarian systems of government. Modi's challenge is to push reform in a noisy democracy. And yet, there is nothing unobjectionable about any of the six points. Many of Modi's political challenges could be solved if he partners closely with chief ministers, many of who are from regional parties which could provide the necessary parliamentary backing (particularly in the Rajya Sabha where the NDA does not have a majority) to get reform done.

Once the first set of China–Singapore style reforms kicks off and the effects begin to show, Modi can move on to implementing parts of the Reagan–Thatcher agenda, like privatisation and complete financial sector deregulation.

But that is more likely to be the programme of a second Modi government should it win again in 2019. In term one, the government will play a big role, hopefully in a much more efficient manner than it did under the UPA, more like Deng and Lee than Manmohan and Sonia.

(This article was first published in *Firstpost.com*)

MODI AND THE SUPREMACY OF LAW

This article was first published in April 2017. Modi's effort to clean up India's warts on a systemic scale continue.

Several years ago, when I was a graduate student in Economics at the University of Cambridge, I recall participating in a discussion about the rise of East Asia's Tiger Economies, still a fashionable subject in the early 2000s. One participant made an unusual point while comparing Singapore and Hong Kong (already at per capita income levels of advanced economies) with China (which was only beginning to shine). All three were populated largely by Han Chinese and none was a democracy in a true sense; all variations of authoritarian regimes. However, according to the participant, the reason Singapore and Hong Kong had thrived and China would continue as before was that the former had inherited the concept of 'rule of law' from the British, something which was alien to mainland Chinese more than a decade after their shift to capitalism. For the uninitiated, he gave a simple example to illustrate the difference. In mainland China, if an individual violated a traffic law and was flagged down by a policeman, an argument would ensue, followed by a gathering of a mob, followed by the hasty departure of the policeman. The offender was right, not the law. In contrast, in Hong Kong and

Singapore, traffic rules were generally obeyed and offenders punished. His argument applied to the law in general.

Most countries that have advanced economies adhere to the rule of law, which means that the law of the land is supreme and no individual, government or judge is above it. Indeed, everyone is subservient to it, particularly government officials. This creates a predictable, conducive and trouble-free environment for all manner of activity, including economic. In December 2016, I was reminded of that discussion at Cambridge fifteen years ago. In India, just about everyone encroaches on the law. The honourable judges of the Supreme Court decided to curb drunken driving by imposing a ban on the sale of liquor within 500 metres of a National Highway. But drunken driving is already against the law and if its rule were supreme, no further intervention would be necessary. Ordinary Indian citizens think nothing of trampling on the law. Few have any fear of the consequences. Being inebriated at the wheel is just one example. Vigilante action taken by groups of various hues is another. If there is a law that exists, it should be enough to either deter violators or punish them. Citizens do not need to enforce justice. People could argue that it is decades of poor governance which has created a culture and incentive system where the rule of law doesn't matter. If a bribe or a connection with someone powerful is enough to sidestep the law with impunity, most individuals would brazenly violate it. Ultimately, it is the pernicious influence of a corrupt, self-enriching, above-the-law executive over a long period that made a mockery of the rule of law even though India, unlike China, did inherit the principle from the British.

But why is it so important to India if China seems to have prospered with scant regard for it? Two reasons. China has an extraordinary State capacity which has delivered high-quality public goods and simultaneously succeeded in suppressing wages and labour. The combination provided an attractive destination for investment, particularly of the global kind, which was looking for alternatives to high-cost advanced economies and rising-wage East Asian Tigers. India does not have a great deal of State capacity, as is evident in the relatively poor state of infrastructure and public goods. India's democracy would not allow an artificial suppression of workers or their wages (note how difficult it is to even mention labour law reforms) and open competition between diverse interest groups in a country that is so heterogeneous (unlike Han-dominated China). The Indian State has thus leant towards uninhibited populism, which tends to destroy rather than foster economic growth.

In India, given the deterioration in institutions that safeguard the rule of law, only strong and decisive leadership can reverse the trend.

The second reason is equally important. While China has achieved much, its per capita income at about 6,000 US dollars is still a fraction of what it is in the West, Singapore and Hong Kong. As the steam runs out of its low-wage, export-based model and China looks to move into higher value-added goods and services, its lack of respect for the rule of law may hurt its prospects: poor protection of intellectual property rights, weak contract enforcement, an opaque financial system and a corrupt political establishment may yet trip or stall China's rise. India, with an income per head that's not even thirty per cent of China's, cannot afford to stumble at all. The country has already witnessed what a breakdown in governance—the kind that happened during the UPA-II regime when laws and rules lost their sanctity, can do to economic growth.

It will take a massive effort to transform India into a country where the rule of law is supreme. But there are hopeful signs under the leadership of Prime Minister Narendra Modi. It may seem contradictory to expect so much of an individual when the entire point is to ensure that individuals in government and the judiciary do not acquire 'larger than law' roles. However, in India, given the deterioration in institutions that safeguard the rule of law, only strong and decisive leadership can reverse the trend. The prime minister has special moral authority because of his personal integrity. Unlike a lot of politicians, he doesn't view himself or his ministerial colleagues as above the law, as shown by his decision to stamp out VIP culture by abolishing the use of red beacons. They must play by the rules. His wider drive against entrenched corruption, including the drastic step of demonetisation, is a radical effort to get all Indians—particularly the non-salaried—to play by the rules. Early evidence suggests that a reasonable number have been nudged to come clean. The rest will be made to face the law. Even a campaign like Swachh Bharat is nudging citizens to take their duties as seriously as their rights and to respect the rule of law.

Fighting and eliminating corruption or exhorting people to do their duty are important steps in restoring the rule of law, but not the only ones. In the end, the government must withdraw from the plethora of interventions it makes, particularly in the economy, many with the noblest of intentions but disastrous in outcomes. Prime Minister Modi is the first leader who has openly committed himself to the maxim of 'Minimum Government, Maximum Governance'. Minimum government would have the State withdraw from unnecessary activity in the regulatory space, the kind which tends to result in violations of the law. The government's commitment to the 'ease of doing business' is essentially about creating a conducive environment for investors.

All the government has to do is ensure a level playing field by letting the rule of law prevail without distortionary interventions. The damage that was done by the UPA enacting a retrospective amendment of tax laws in the Vodafone case would never happen in an economy governed this way. In the end, State capacity to deliver public goods, still an important goal for India (the maximum governance bit) will be achieved when bureaucrats focus on doing their real jobs—of drafting sound legislation and implementing parliamentary enactments—and not meddling needlessly in spheres which do not require their attention. The same applies to judges, who must interpret the law to uphold its supremacy instead of turning legislative themselves (even with the best of intentions).

Prime Minister Modi's lasting legacy to India's economy and indeed polity should be an assurance that it never needs another Modi to rescue it from the abyss. In countries where the rule of law prevails, individual politicians, bureaucrats and judges can do only limited damage. Modi, with his personal integrity, commitment to minimum government, aversion to careless populism, and vision of all-inclusive growth is best positioned to make the rule of law supreme. India needs *Sabka saath, sabka vikaas* and *sabka kanoon.*

(This article was first published in the *Open* magazine.)

MISSION: LESS-CASH ECONOMY

This article was first published in December 2016 when, in the aftermath of demonetisation, scepticism was growing about the possibility of India becoming less addicted to cash. This article countered the scepticism by arguing that the foundations for a less-cash, digital economy had been laid in the five years that led up to November 2016. Demonetisation was the catalyst which nudged change. Twenty-three months on, the use of digital payments has grown hugely.

It is perfectly reasonable to be sceptical about a less-cash Indian economy, if you still live in 2010. What the cynics seemed to have missed is that rapid technological change, well harnessed by both the public and private sectors, has laid a foundation on which a cashless—or for the sake of the purists, a less-cash economy (no economy will ever be completely cashless)—can be built relatively quickly.

The foundation rests on four pillars. The first pillar is Aadhaar which has given a unique biometric identity to over one billion Indians, a feat unique to India. And it is to Nandan Nilekani's credit that he managed to build Aadhaar, with great efficiency between 2009 and 2014, as a government-project while successfully negotiating the obstructionist tendencies of the system.

The second pillar was built just as the first neared completion. Prime Minister Narendra Modi's Jan Dhan Yojana, announced in 2014, has enabled ninety-eight per cent of India's households to have access to a bank account. This statistic is not government data. Instead, it is provided by a survey from an independent agency, PRICE (People's Research on India's Consumer Economy).

Meanwhile, the third and fourth pillars—smartphone penetration and ever cheaper connectivity—were being laid outside the government. Rapid improvements in technology and scale to manufacture mobile phones, particularly smartphones, has led to a sharp drop in prices and increased ownership. Already, India has 220 million smartphone users (in 2010, this number was twenty million), which is estimated to rise to over 700 million by 2020.

The fourth pillar is the evolution of competition in the telecom sector, which has pushed prices for mobile telephony and data usage sharply downwards—the entry of Reliance Jio in early 2016 seriously altered the competition dynamics in favour of consumers.

Despite a solid foundation, it would have needed a serious nudge for an economy used to functioning overwhelmingly on cash to move to a less-cash system. Demonetisation is more a shock than a nudge. Its primary objectives may have been a crackdown on tax evasion and corruption. But any achievement of those objectives needs a decisive move away from cash transactions. Of course, if demonetisation had been announced in 2010, there would have been no alternative platform to conduct transactions easily and critics could have had a field day. But now there is a real, solid foundation.

Needless to say, much more work remains to be done. And the four pillars of a less-cash economy need the full support of the other four Ps—public–private–personal partnership—to succeed. The perception about demonetisation and the campaign for a less-cash economy is that it is highly Delhi-centric with the Union Government trying to enforce change like in the old days of central planning. Nothing could be farther from the truth.

The drive to move to less-cash is devolved down to the lowest tier of government, whether panchayats or Collectors/ District Magistrates, who are championing change. Most recently, four panchayats in the districts of Bokaro and East Singbum reported going cashless (what they meant was to a very high degree of digitisation, with bank account, smartphone and payment apps, access to all households) thus setting an example for others to follow.

Therefore, the public sector in this entire exercise needs to be understood as all tiers of government, with the lowest tier being the most important.

Similarly, private sector participation in the making of a less-cash economy isn't only about big telecom companies or providers of digital wallets. It is about the entire private sector, particularly its smallest elements like retailers and traders, moving to accepting payments by digital methods. Again, because of the technological feasibility and low costs, this is not an impossibility. The government is already playing a helping hand by providing tax and other incentives for this.

A public–private partnership won't succeed without the personal. Individuals all over India need to take a leaf out of the book of the villagers of Bokaro and East Singbum and make an effort to change habits. The fact is that if the cynics are right and that only a very small minority of India (not more than five per cent) holds cash because it indulges in illicit activities like tax evasion and corruption, then there is all the more reason to expect the actions of the 'personal' overall (or ninety-five per cent of individuals) to align with the 'public' and 'private' to graduate India to a less-cash economy.

India has a long habit of defying conventional wisdom and the naysayers. It's time for India's Rip Van Winkles to wake up and smell the possibilities.

(This article was first published in the *DNA*.)

BANKING ON THE PERSONAL SECTOR

This article was first published in May 2017 when Modi's government completed three years in office. Among the other changes ushered in by Modi, this piece highlights the fact that Modi has been able to remind citizens of their own roles and duties in transforming India.

According to conventional wisdom, the first three years of a government's five-year term is the time for radical policy changes, particularly of the kind which may not have a mass constituency in the short term but are necessary in the interest of long-term transformation. The last two years are usually earmarked for popular and populist announcements. Prime Minister Narendra Modi abides rarely by either conventional wisdom or pre-written scripts. After all, circa May 2014, who would have predicted that demonetisation would be the most radical (at least in the 'big bang' sense) policy measure of the first three years?

In India, the process of reform and transformation isn't about a big bang or two, but a steady workman-like approach to changing a dysfunctional policy ecosystem. In fact, Modi may be close to untying the Gordian knot of India's chronic under-performance by bringing clarity and credibility to the muddled thinking on the relative roles of the State and capitalism/free markets in the country's economic development.

There are some good reasons and some bad reasons for India's mixed-up economy. In 1947, it wasn't unreasonable for the founding fathers to lean towards a greater role for the State in the economy. Until then, free markets were a symbol of exploitative colonialism and a country ravaged by it for two centuries had limited resources and capacity for the private sector to take the lead. Things went horribly wrong in the 1960s when India took a sharp Left turn towards autarky and ever greater State control over the economy just as the future Tiger Economies of East Asia were opening up. It's never too late to make a decisive change as China showed in the years after it opened up to free markets in 1978. Unfortunately, India's liberalisation in 1991 was borne out of necessity and not conviction. While some parts of the economy were freed up between 1991 and 1996 and then between 1998 and 2004, too many areas of the economy were still controlled or dominated by an unreformed State apparatus. What India got was an unparalleled (by domestic standards) boom in growth rates between 2003 and 2012 accompanied by a virulent strain of crony capitalism which threatened to destroy the legitimacy of free markets and, therefore, erode even the limited foundation India had for prosperity.

When Prime Minister Narendra Modi took office in 2014, India's growth rate had slipped to distinctly pre-liberalisation levels of the sub-five per cent kind. There was a crisis within the mighty government apparatus characterised internally by policy paralysis, indecision and deep uncertainty, and outwardly by rampant scams and spiralling inflation. And there was a crisis in markets, with public perception of India's capitalists and businessmen at a low not seen since the peak of statism.

For the India story to regain its lustre, it would need extraordinary leadership to first pull out of the morass and then, second, to relay the foundation for a sustainable, rapid growth into the future. Prime Minister Modi embodied a unique set of qualities and qualifications which would enable him to set the stage for India's turnaround. At a personal level, his rise to the top was based on merit and hard work, and not nepotism and dynastic succession characteristic of many of the politicians who had presided over grinding India to a halt. His reputation for probity and personal integrity made him stand out in a political class which had long used politics as a means of self-enrichment and enrichment of cronies.

His personal qualities were supplemented by his professional accomplishments. He had spent twelve years in office as chief minister of Gujarat, a period in which the state recorded China-like double-digit growth rates and not just in industry where it always had a comparative advantage but also in agriculture where it quite clearly did not. Underlying the phenomenal economic performance of Gujarat was a philosophy or a mode of governance, which he would use in New Delhi. There was nothing muddled or mixed up about it. The State had a clear role; in building state-of-the-art infrastructure and investing in the poor (not via doles or careless populism). Free markets and entrepreneurship had a clear role whether in building industry or farming more productively. The interface between the State and markets, that troublesome swamp of rent-seeking and corruption, was cleaned up by ushering in greater transparency, particularly through the use of the most modern technology available. Every successful economy has to find the right mix of the State and markets to prosper. The Gujarat model had created a Guangdong in western India under the overarching policy framework set by the Union Government which was identical for all of India. It differentiated itself by showing impressive state capacity (for implementation), unleashing and encouraging entrepreneurship and using the policy autonomy granted to the states of India under the Constitution to create a better policy environment for double-digit growth.

The combined power of Modi's personal stature and his accomplishments and clarity as an administrator accompanied him into prime ministerial office in May 2014. Modi's unique attributes and their translation into governance defined his first three years in office. No doubt, if he wins a second term, the track towards transformation will not change. Young India is impatient for rapid change, and that is a good thing, but transformations take a while to materialise once the foundation is put in place. Remember, that even China took at least ten to fifteen years after the 1978 reforms, just as the fruits of the reforms between 1991 and 1996, and 1998 and 2004 flowered in the years that followed.

Consider how the foundation has been shaped. First, the role of the government. At the core of the commitment to minimum government is fiscal responsibility and a stable macroeconomic environment characterised by low and stable inflation. Also at the core of righting the role of the State is the promise to improve India's ranking in the World Bank's Ease of Doing Business survey. Getting here requires getting the bureaucracy out of areas it has unnecessarily waded into over the years. At the same time, there is a commitment to maximum governance which means that the government must do more efficiently and transparently its work in building critical infrastructure, whether physical or social. It must also carry out its core functions of maintaining law and order and defence in an efficient manner. For these areas, there is no compromise on spending where necessary. There has been an unequivocal move to reduce discretion on the part of government officials wherever possible through the use of technology or superior management methods. It isn't possible to wish the State away in India but it is possible to reorient its role. That is happening, most noticeably in the government's fight against poverty. The flagship schemes of Modi's government are designed for investing in the poor and not giving doles. Hence, the three schemes for subsidised insurance (life, accident and crop failure). The Ujjwala scheme has empowered the poorest households to use LPG instead of health-destroying fuels and cooking methods. Modi has even managed to persuade crores of middle-class Indians to give up their undeserved subsidy for LPG voluntarily. Even an old scheme like MGNREGA has been reoriented to the building of productive assets so that the money spent yields genuine returns.

Importantly, building from his experience as chief minister, Modi views state governments as partners rather than supplicants in the development process. Constitutionally, several subjects are in the domain of states and so no transformation is possible in the absence of serious reform by the states.

In the environment of 2014, it would have been tempting for any politician to create a backlash against markets and capitalists. However, Modi chose a different path. He gave no ground on crony capitalism. The disruptive demonetisation exercise was a strong message to crony capitalists, tax evaders and other sundry individuals who refused to do business by the rules of the game. At the same time, renegotiating bilateral tax treaties with foreign countries was a way to ensure that black money is not stashed abroad easily. The war on black money and illegitimate capitalism will continue but not at the cost of genuine entrepreneurship. Hence, policies like Make in India, Startup India and Stand-up India, easing of FDI norms across sectors to facilitate new and existing entrepreneurs. The prime minister is acutely aware that the creation of jobs on the scale required by the workforce will only happen by the flourishing of entrepreneurship. The implementation of the Goods and Services Tax is also a pro-market measure which will ease many of the obstacles faced by businesses (including abolishing the notorious octroi) while bringing benefits to consumers and the government in the form of greater tax revenues.

It is Prime Minister Modi's ability to create a conducive ecosystem for economic growth and a win-win scenario for all key stakeholders that will eventually define his leadership of India. In fact, he has treaded into turf beyond just the public (State) and private (market) to facilitate change. Unusually for an Indian leader, he has exhorted society or the 'personal' sector to play its role in the transformation of India. He has shown us the mirror with Swachh Bharat and demonetisation. The reality is that if India is to transform, the government must reform, the private sector must clean up its act and individuals must begin to be responsible and do their duties (by not littering or by paying taxes, to take just two examples). By 2019, this unique public–private–personal partnership would have put India on the cusp of transformation from the verge of despair in 2014. By 2022 or 2024, the seeds of change will begin to flower into the fruits of prosperity.

(This article was first published in the *Open* magazine.)

SEIZE THE ASIAN CENTURY

This article was first published in January 2018. It argues that Modi must seize the opportunity to preserve an open, liberal, and global economic order.

Eighteen years ago, as the millennium drew to a close, the annual ministerial meeting of the World Trade Organisation in Seattle in the US was derailed by the fury of thousands of street protestors denouncing the forces of globalisation and the governments which represented them. Last month, at the dusk of 2017, a ministerial meeting of the WTO in Buenos Aires, Argentina ended in a whimper with the US leading a general apathy towards free trade and globalisation. Perhaps 2017 will be remembered as the year when the liberal economic consensus on free markets and globalisation was finally buried in its homelands, the US and UK. One wonders though what the street protesters of Seattle make of the cast of characters administering the last rites to the 'Washington Consensus'. Not Fidel Castro or Hugo Chavez or even Lula da Silva but instead a Republican President of the US, who also happens to be a billionaire, and a powerful faction of the Conservative Party of the UK. For the global Left, the 'victory' must be bittersweet.

For ordinary citizens of the world, the ideological and policy shifts in the advanced economies, particularly post-Trump America and post-Brexit Britain, are likely to be more bitter than sweet. Consider the view from emerging economies. No other period in human history has seen as many people lifted out of absolute poverty as in the three decades since the mid-1980s. That is largely because the world's two most populous nations, China and India, made rapid strides in terms of economic growth in this period.

China, which embraced openness and internal reform more vigorously than India, has been the bigger beneficiary. India, with its limited openness and gradual internal reform process, registered lower growth than China but higher growth rates than any other point in its history. It would be cynical to say that the forces of globalisation and free markets have only enriched a minority in these countries. The fact is that more than half a billion people have been lifted out of poverty in a single generation by the very forces that are now being buried in the countries of their origin.

This is not to argue that there were no flaws in the system. The role of Wall Street and global finance in bringing disrepute to the system is well known. That is what precipitated the 2008 financial crisis which sowed the seeds for a backlash. But curiously, politics has chosen to target free trade and free (only relatively) movement of labour, soft targets compared to the powerful world of finance. There is a grave danger for both emerging economies and advanced economies with this form of backlash.

In the advanced economies, it is convenient to blame free trade for job losses in manufacturing, without commenting on the huge benefits such trade has brought for consumers who are clearly better off as a result of cheaper products and services.

It is easy to target immigrants without acknowledging the huge value-add they bring to the host economies. Think of the number of foreign-born persons in top positions in American or British academia or in Silicon Valley. Without them, the US (even the UK) would not be so wealthy. Any sustained backlash against free trade and immigration will ultimately hurt the economic and geo-political interests of the US and the UK.

Still, the advanced economies may be wealthy enough to delay the day of reckoning. For countries like India and several other emerging and developing economies, a closed world means missed opportunities and a longer journey out of poverty for those who continue to remain poor. They have the most important stake in ensuring that the world doesn't return to wealth-destroying autarky.

Pegged to Reforms

However, before batting for openness abroad, emerging economies need to put their houses in order. For many emerging economies, particularly China and India, the backlash against free markets isn't likely to stem from external considerations (free trade or free movement of labour), but from a free market system at home that has been vitiated by crony capitalism. It isn't surprising that the leaders of both China and India, President Xi Jinping and Prime Minister Narendra Modi, have devoted a considerable amount of political capital to combat corruption and root out entrenched vested interests. It isn't an easy task and it won't happen overnight but the battle against corruption and cronyism is a critical element in retaining the legitimacy of an open market economy which has delivered more prosperity than any alternative system in the last hundred years. In India, the battle against graft has to be accompanied by an attempt to improve State capacity, because there are certain critical functions which only the State can perform.

Reform at home must be accompanied by a willingness to open up to the rest of the world. China has been aggressive about exports and about attracting foreign investment but has been more protectionist about imports (particularly services and agricultural goods) and its State-owned enterprises. India has never quite embraced an export-oriented development strategy. Somehow the point that the domestic market is large enough has won the argument even when it is apparent that the global market is several times that size. Just the global market for merchandise trade is eighteen trillion US dollars, almost nine times the size of India's total GDP. India needs to capture a much larger share of that market than its present 1.6 per cent share. India also needs to capture a greater share of foreign investment. But for that to happen, it needs to give up its traditionally defensive posture on trade in particular. The opportunity has never been better as China's wages rise and it reorients its economic strategy from primarily an export-led growth to a more consumption-driven economy.

India and China hold the key to the emerging global political economy. Joining the US and other advanced economies in closing up will only lead to slower growth. The challenge for India and China, as the two fastest growing major economies, is to engage with each other and with other willing partner nations, particularly in the East Asia and the Pacific region (including advanced economies like Japan and Australia), to maintain openness and embrace globalisation. The Regional Comprehensive Economic Partnership (RCEP) is one forum where this engagement can happen. India can engage on free trade and free investment in other groups like the BBIN (Bangladesh, Bhutan, India, Nepal) and BIMSTEC (Bangladesh, India, Myanmar, Sri Lanka, Nepal, Thailand, Bhutan) and via these groups with the entire ASEAN region.

The scenario is set for an Asian century. But for it to materialise, India, China and the rest of the region need to look beyond rivalry and defensiveness to explore the possibilities of economic integration as the West, so dominant for the last two hundred years, marginalises and isolates itself. That is the promise of 2018 and beyond.

(This article was first published in *The Hindu*.)

DIVIDENDS OF DISRUPTION

This article was first published in November 2017. It was written on the first anniversary of demonetisation and argued that the withdrawal of high currency notes by Prime Minister Modi was a very twenty-first century positive disruption of the status quo which would yield big gains.

In the twenty-first century, disruption is the key to advance and progress. In the English language, that may sound counter-intuitive. As it might for practitioners of government in India. India's State apparatus has been a great disruptor for the last seventy years, across two centuries—in the cause of progress, for the goal of advance. The disruptive, interventionist and interfering administrative and policy practices of the Indian State date back to the nineteenth century. As does the traditional definition of 'disruption'. Today, it isn't about value destruction. It is about a new creativity with the potential to transform lives. The only thing in common between the disruption of the old and the new is that there will be a set of losers. In the new disruption, many more will be winners. New technology may destroy some old jobs, but it will create newer, better ones. Narendra Modi is India's first twenty-first century politician, the pioneer who embraced the technologies and possibilities of the first fifteen years of the century while his peers stood frozen in the old world. Unsurprisingly, Modi understands the power of disruption as well as its consequences. If he did not, it is highly unlikely that demonetisation would have been announced on the evening of 8 November 2016.

Those who damn demonetisation as 'flawed economics' or 'populist politics' fail to grasp the power of a disruptive idea and its consequences. When Prime Minister Modi said that the withdrawal of high-value currency notes (or eighty-six per cent of the total circulation) was intended to strike a blow on black money, counterfeit currency and terrorism, he did not mean that any of the three would disappear overnight or even in a matter of months. Black money (and the parallel economy), counterfeiting and money-laundering for terror-related activities had entrenched themselves deeply, creating power constituencies across business (big and small), politics (national, regional, local), various mafia and groups of ordinary citizens who depended on the rotten system to deliver basic necessities.

It is easy to argue that several measures other than demonetisation ought to be used to tackle these problems. Indeed, several have been deployed over the years, but none of these, by themselves, is sufficient to dislodge such a well-entrenched system of *mala fide* activity. The perpetrators could always be rest assured that the government would not come after them with all its might. Until the evening demonetisation was announced.

Unlike any other measure, it would directly affect every resident of India, without exception. It was not aimed at any particular constituency or set of constituencies. It was highly risky for the government, as a majority of residents who did not possess any black money and who were law-abiding would face hardship in the short term. It also entailed risk because there was every possibility that there would be no immediate gains—they would instead accrue over time—whereas the hardship would be immediate. It was very popular, if opinion polls and the UP election were accurate indicators, despite the criticism it received from sundry pundits.

The critique of demonetisation has centred around the fact that some 99.5 per cent of the demonetised currency found its way into bank accounts. Therefore, no black money was destroyed and thus demonetisation failed in its primary stated objective. Of course, it would have been ideal if a substantial amount of black money was simply destroyed, but it was always unrealistic to expect vested interests to part with their wealth so easily. The manner in which several banks or their employees colluded with black money holders was only added evidence on how deeply embedded the parallel economy was.

However, critics choose to overlook the fact that not all the money deposited into bank accounts automatically becomes legitimate. Importantly, demonetisation may have induced a behavioural change in citizens. The number of new persons filing tax returns has gone up sharply post-demonetisation. An additional 5.6 million persons filed Income Tax returns between April and August 2017. A number of people also availed of the amnesty scheme that the government offered. In addition, several other suspicious accounts are being scrutinised and taxes and penalties imposed. Overall, 1.8 million accounts have been found with average deposits above 2.5 lakh rupees where the account holder's deposits do not match their income profile. There can be little doubt that many more Indians are now in the tax net after demonetisation, either voluntarily or involuntarily. This is critical in a country that has an abysmally low tax-GDP ratio of around seventeen per cent, which is half the average of developed countries. Given the country's spending requirements on infrastructure, both physical and social, increasing the tax base is potentially transformative.

The other lasting transformative effect of demonetisation is its nudge towards a less-cash, digitally-driven economy. Again, it is not a transformation which will happen right away, but there is no denying that people who would otherwise have never used digital transactions are now doing so. Significantly, there seems to have been a structural shift in favour of digital payments even though the number of such transactions may have fallen from their peak once the economy was remonetised. A paper by Rupa Subramanya, economist and journalist, for the Observer Research Foundation (March 2017) crunches several data sources to conclude a behavioural change, adding much-needed rigour to a debate that has too often taken place in the absence of evidence.

The structural shift towards digital payments is quite intuitive. Everyone who was using cash wasn't doing so to avoid taxes, though a small minority may have done. A big majority of Indians were simply not exposed to the possibilities and instruments of easy and cheap digital transactions. Demonetisation not only nudged people to try out digital mechanisms, but also led to innovations in the digital payments space which have enabled people to transact easily and at low cost. The BHIM app developed by the government is only one such example.

There was always bound to be noisy opposition to demonetisation, given that it would strike at the roots of firmly entrenched vested interests. Several economists provided intellectual cover by succumbing to their professional obsession with the short run—sorry John Maynard Keynes, but there is a long run in which we are alive! Those economists argued that demonetisation would lead to a drastic fall in economic activity, in particular damaging small businesses and wage labour, the most vulnerable stakeholders in the economy. Indeed, there was short-run disruption, though clearly not of the catastrophic scale prophesised by the measure's opponents. And it is precisely the most vulnerable stakeholders of the economy who pay the heaviest price of the old order characterised by corruption and tax evasion.

In October 2017, American economist Richard Thaler won the Nobel Prize for his research in the domain of behavioural economics, a relatively new branch of the discipline which eschews some of the assumptions of mainstream economics and gives more weight to frailties in human decision-making. While there was a raging debate (at least on social media) on how fully Thaler supported demonetisation, he did acknowledge its potential in nudging people to change their behaviour, something which seems to be happening. Clearly, the practitioners of this new economics, along with the practitioners of technology and innovation understand the power of disruption to alter the normal course of history.

It isn't common for governments to get disruptions right anywhere in the world. Historically, market forces and technology have combined to do it better. Market forces have not been able to disrupt India's deep-rooted corruption. If anything, post-1991, India's vested interests took over market forces, unleashing virulent crony capitalism. To even begin to uproot the old order would have required a bold intervention. Prime Minister Modi unleashed a dramatic disruption. In doing so, he has sent out a clear signal that India's future trajectory will be different from its past. It will be cleaner, fairer and faster. And while cheering for a better future, for once no one will shed tears for the losers—tax evaders, crony capitalists, counterfeiters—from a disruption.

(This article was first published in the *Open* magazine.)

PM SHOWS INDIA THE MIRROR

This piece was first published in August 2014, a day after Modi's first Independence Day speech as prime minister. In the speech he exhorted all citizens to own responsibility for change, a theme he has reiterated through his term in office.

It has always been a favourite, almost obsessive pastime of India to show its politicians a mirror which reveals their ugly face—corrupt, incompetent and self-serving. Now, finally, a politician has shown India a mirror which reveals an almost equally ugly face—disrespecting of women, filthy and totally self-serving. It needed someone with the confidence of a Narendra Modi to admonish a constantly self-pitying citizenry. And he was heard without a whimper of protest.

The fact is that both India's rulers and its ruled had got used to living in a political economy of entitlements. The dynasts for long believed that they had a right to be the ruling class. In turn, they would provide entitlements to the impoverished masses—from free food to free schooling to doles. It might well have been a cosy and functional arrangement, except that the rulers failed to adequately deliver the promised entitlements to the citizenry. The voters obliged the 'entitled' rulers with their votes, but got little in return. They had every right to be angry and show their leaders a mirror. The rulers could never, not with any legitimacy anyway, admonish the citizens for their many failings.

Clearly, Modi wants to change the entrenched relationship between the ruler and the ruled. He is uniquely positioned to do so. He was never 'entitled' to rule. If anything, he was always considered unfit to rule by the entrenched ruling class (which would have been happy with any mainstream alternative to Modi within the BJP). He has risen to the top overcoming several obstacles, many of which involved reforming his own personality and attitude. Modi has little patience for a citizenry which expects the government to spoon-feed it. He will simply not allow all of India's failures to be placed at the door of his government. Society and individuals will have to share the blame for failure, while also sharing the credit for success.

Of course, this doesn't mean that the State will withdraw from the public sphere. By all accounts, Modi will strive to strengthen the functioning of government and improve the quality of services that government agencies deliver to the citizenry.

But can women's empowerment be the job of the State alone? No, society must play ball. Nobody can argue against the fact that the law and order machinery has to be overhauled to ensure that crimes against women are prevented and prosecuted more efficiently than now. But can the law and order machinery alone eliminate violence against women? It will always be tough for any law enforcement to prevent female foeticide. Modi is on the right track by demanding that the people at large also take responsibility for progressive change.

India cannot claim to be a modern society when so many of its citizens live in squalor. Again, sanitation is in part the responsibility of the government, and the previous governments haven't done enough for it. But can the State really prevent people from spitting in public places? Or prevent people from using public spaces as urinals? Perhaps, if the State is draconian in its punishment, like in Singapore. But in India, where we are rightly proud of our greater liberalism, citizens need to be aware of their duties.

Citizens in a democracy have rights, but they also have duties. India has always been vocal about its rights, and that's a good thing. But now, under the leadership of Modi, both politicians and citizens are reminded of their duties. The era of easy entitlements without responsibility is at an end. Both politicians and citizens need to pass the ugly mirror test.

(This article was first published in *The Sunday Guardian*.)

THE GEOGRAPHY OF CHANGE

This article was first published in January 2017 in the run up to elections to the state of Manipur. But it makes a broader argument about transformation of India's Northeast as a consequence of Modi's Act East Policy.

It is the least talked about election in the national media, even though it is going to take place in the most fraught circumstances. Manipur is set to go to the polls with Uttar Pradesh, Punjab, Uttarakhand, and Goa in February and March amidst an economic blockade that has paralysed parts of the state, including Imphal. It is a situation stereotypical of the Northeast—an unstable, unrest-prone region that's distant, isolated and presided over by opportunist politicians looking for more and more aid from New Delhi, and of only limited relevance to mainstream India. In Manipur, history seems to repeat itself as tragedy only too frequently. However, for the Northeast, and this doesn't exclude Manipur, the time is particularly fortuitous to break away from the stereotype. The rising economic trajectory of Asia, positive political changes in India's neighbourhood and a Union Government that is determined to 'Act East', mean that now's the moment to begin rewriting the old narrative.

There are, of course, good reasons for the real backwardness of the Northeast as well as for the perceived need for special, almost hand-holding, treatment. History dealt the Northeastern states a harsh hand in 1947 when the Partition of India and the separation of East Pakistan left these states with only a tiny corridor (the Chicken's Neck in northern West Bengal) linking them with the rest of India. At one stroke, from being an integral part of what was at the time the most connected region in the world (apart from the region which is today India, Pakistan and Bangladesh, Burma {now, Myanmar} too was a part of the British Empire), India's Northeast was caught in a tricky geography; in addition to difficult hilly terrain in most of the region, it was set to become isolated from the rest of India and from relatively easy access to the coast (via East Pakistan). After Independence, the hostility of China, the insularity of Burma and the tension with Pakistan ensured that the region had little opportunity to connect, at least in economic terms, with the world outside. An accident of history and the curse of geography destined the region to an embrace with backwardness. And it provided fertile ground for the numerous insurgencies and violence which plunged the region into even deeper isolation.

Almost seventy years have passed since Independence and the attitudes in Delhi and in the Northeast remain remarkably static—mired in a backwardness, isolationist and 'special treatment' paradigm. For Delhi's security establishment, border regions have been viewed, with justifiable reason, as zones of 'threat' and 'terror' and not of opportunity and prosperity. A difficult neighbourhood has meant that the word most commonly suffixed to cross-border is 'terror', not trade. Unsurprisingly, the states of the Northeast are hubs for the military and not manufacturing. Visiting some of these states still requires Inner Line Permits, even for Indian nationals. Delhi's economic policy establishment is guiltier than the security establishment. Instead of promoting trade and connectivity in border regions, India's economic policy mandarins have long viewed trade with suspicion. Even after the liberalisation of 1991, India's economic bureaucracy is yet to fully accept that freer trade is an engine of growth and prosperity. A glance at the number of restrictions on the products that can be traded across the border over land is a constant reminder of the persistence of the old mindset.

That said, the region's political leadership must also share the blame for an unchanging narrative. The fracas led by the chief ministers and assorted political parties in 2015 over the recommendations of the 14th Finance Commission which seemed to do away with 'Special Category' status for the Northeast, and which only turned out to be a change in nomenclature, was indicative. These states continue to receive financial assistance on more generous 'special' terms than other Indian states (barring the hill states).

The narrative needs to change from security, sops and special status to one of investment, opportunity and growth. Now is the perfect time because history and geography have changed sides presenting India's Northeast with a unique opportunity for an economic take off.

History isn't always made at one stroke, like in 1947. The history of the world, particularly Asia, has evolved slowly but considerably over the last few decades. The big trends favour India, particularly the Northeast. In the last seven decades, the most remarkable economic take-off stories of all times have been scripted east of India: first in Japan, then in North-East Asia and the Asian Tigers (South Korea, Taiwan, Hong Kong, Singapore), then in South-East Asia (what we now know as the ASEAN), and finally in China. Many of these countries, most famously Korea, were viewed as basket cases in 1953 before they emerged as world beaters in just three decades. Significantly, each of the East Asian latecomers used openness and connectivity (cross-border trade and investment) as the key tools to achieve rapid prosperity. The integration has been within the region as much as with the rest of the world. Until India began its own rise to rapid growth in the early 2000s, East Asia was the fastest growing region in the world. In 2016, India is the planet's fastest growing major economy, but China and ASEAN are next on that count (and at much higher income levels). At the same time, growth rates in the US, Europe and Japan have either been falling or stagnant or only marginally positive in the last decade and more. The world's prosperity engine is South and East Asia. The Northeast of India sits at the centre, or at the crossroads, of the rest of India and East Asia. It has to exploit its new geography at the centre of the world's pole of growth to achieve its own take off.

Recent trends in India's neighbourhood have also increased opportunities for the Northeast. The gradual opening up of Myanmar over the last decade and the installation of a democratic pro-India government (which is viewed as an important counterweight to China's overbearing presence) is a huge boon. The development of major routes of connectivity over land from India's Northeast through Myanmar to Thailand and other ASEAN countries (the Asian trilateral highway is one such project) could boost trade and economic activity in the Northeast significantly. If Myanmar provides the opening to markets in South-East Asia, then Bangladesh, which also has a pro-India government in office, is ready to provide a corridor back into the rest of India, as well as into an economy which is growing impressively. States like Tripura and Meghalaya, which have only indirect and long routed access to the rest of India have much better access to Bangladesh and to the rest of India through that country. To take an example, it is just a three-hour drive from Agartala to Dhaka or a four-and-a-half hour run from Agartala to the Bangladesh port of Chittagong, whereas it would take an entire day to drive from Agartala to Guwahati, the closest commercial hub in India. Manipur is next door to Myanmar. The distance from Imphal to Guwahati is just under 500 km and the distance from Imphal to Mandalay, Myanmar's second biggest city, is just over 550 kms. Next door Myanmar is an easy gateway to the lucrative ASEAN market.

Politics in New Delhi is also more favourable to the Northeast than at any time in the recent past. Prime Minister Narendra Modi has laid special emphasis on the development of India's laggard eastern and North-eastern regions. He has also shifted a gear on India's East Asia policy from 'Look East' to 'Act East'. South Asian regional integration, a perennial non-starter because of India–Pakistan tensions, may finally be getting a boost through sub-regional arrangements. The Bangladesh, Bhutan, India, Nepal (BBIN) initiative is important. Its members signed a motor vehicle agreement in 2015 that would allow vehicles of each country to ply in the other, a prerequisite for efficient trade over land. A re-emphasis of the BIMSTEC initiative, which links sub-regional South Asia with sub-regional South-East Asia, is a significant opportunity for India's Northeast (and for India as a whole).

All of these developments—in the economies of East Asia and India, in the governments of key neighbouring countries, and in the Government of India—have created a unique moment in history. The Northeast can occupy the centre-stage. But how?

There is little doubt that the states of the Northeast are relatively backward and constitute a minor part of India's economy. The seven States of the region plus Sikkim have a GDP that's only 2.6 per cent of India's economy. The states account for three per cent of the country's population. There are three facts to be noted that underlie the overall numbers. First, Assam alone accounts for 1.6 per cent of India's GDP; the size of the GSDPs of the other states is much less. Second, in per capita income terms, only Sikkim and Arunachal Pradesh are above the Indian average. Third, taken as a whole the region is indeed a viable economic unit: Myanmar's GDP is the equivalent of 3.2 per cent of India's, only somewhat larger than the Northeast states taken together.

The most obvious constraint to economic growth in the Northeast is the fact that the region is landlocked. It is usually the case that coastal belts achieve prosperity more easily than such regions largely because they have better access to trade. That said, there are examples of landlocked countries which are either prosperous or reasonably so and have very high trade-to-GDP ratios: Switzerland, Austria, the Czech Republic, Botswana and Paraguay. The key to the high trade ratio and economic growth in these countries is close economic integration with neighbouring countries. That alone can make up for the disadvantages of lacking direct access to sea lanes. For the Northeast of India, this would mean closer economic integration with Myanmar and Bangladesh. The fact is that a large proportion of global trade takes place through value chains where value is added to a product across regions and countries. Fortunately for India and its Northeast, East Asia and China are major hubs for such global value chains and there is great scope for integration.

Closer commercial ties call not only for lower tariffs and fewer restrictions on what can be traded across land borders, but also the requisite infrastructure to facilitate trade. What is singularly critical is road connectivity within the region and with neighbouring countries. Rail links have their limitations, given the poor network at present. It takes a long time to lay railway tracks in such difficult terrain, as seen in large parts of the region. Hearteningly, however, several big-ticket highway projects are in the pipeline, and these need to be expedited. But quality roads, while necessary, may not be sufficient. Take the case of agricultural products, both raw and processed, for which the region would have a natural comparative advantage. Apart from transport links, trade requires essential infrastructure like cold chains, laboratories to test for requisite standards, and land customs stations at several border points (a handful exist at present), for it to flourish. The Northeast also has a comparative advantage in minerals and minerals-based industry. For now, coal and limestone are among the commodities that the region exports—mostly to neighbouring countries. Like the rest of India, the Northeast states need to focus on improving the ease of doing business so that greater value addition takes place right there.

The government's strategy of engaging with the CMLV group—Cambodia, Myanmar, Laos and Vietnam—of the most backward countries of ASEAN through two-way cross-border investments, for which it is considering setting up Special Purpose Vehicles, is a logical extension of forging such relationships with the immediate neighbourhood. There are likely to be greater complementarities and less fears of competition from these set of countries than the larger ASEAN region.

For commerce and investment to thrive in any region, the presence of cities or urban agglomerations with their accompanying infrastructure is a necessary condition. The Ministry of Urban Development runs more than one scheme for urban development/ rejuvenation, including the flagship Smart Cities project. Instead of targeting existing cities (particularly in the Northeast), there is every reason to fund the creation of new, smart cities on the borders. The obvious candidates for such investment are Dawki (Meghalaya–Bangladesh), Zemithang (Arunachal Pradesh–China/Bhutan), Sutarkandi (Assam–Bangladesh), Moreh (Manipur–Myanmar), Zokhawthar (Mizoram–Myanmar), and Khowaighat (Tripura–Bangladesh). For now, these are villages or small towns with populations ranging from a few hundred in Dawki and Zemithang to a few thousand in Zokhawthar, Moreh, Khowai and Sutarkandi. These could be transformed into new urban centres that would be India's gateways to the neighbouring countries. The Central and state governments would have to lead this project, but it would make eminent sense to invite participation and investment from the neighbouring countries and East Asia to build world-class townships. Given that these townships will also serve as entry points for neighbours and other East Asian countries to access Indian markets, there is bound to be interest.

The key to their urbanisation is connectivity. They must be linked by highways (at least four-lanes) to the respective state capitals and with highways to one another. Railheads could be a long-term plan, but for now airports could be fast-tracked. The development of six new cities could provide a catalyst for other connectivity projects. But this requires large sums of investment, not simply more generous sponsorship of old schemes by the government.

It is reasonable to ask that given the long history of law and order problems in the Northeast, what are the prospects of real change? Many of the insurgencies that plagued the region right up to the 1980s and 1990s have either ended or significantly ebbed, particularly in Mizoram, Assam and Tripura. These states are ready to capitalise on the new circumstances. Election-bound Manipur remains the most volatile state in the region. Ultimately, the only sustainable solution to this state's problems is connectivity and economic development. There is an urgent need to create constituencies of peace and prosperity (which will come through greater trade and economic integration) to counter those of violence and unrest. Law and order versus economic development is often a chicken-and-egg problem: it is difficult to tell which comes first. But given the relative peace of most of the region, notwithstanding the poll-related trouble in Manipur, now is the best chance to create large constituencies of people who would benefit from economic advance while resisting destructionist forces. It is a matter of viewing the region as an opportunity rather than a challenge, both in New Delhi and in state capitals. For the Northeast, prosperity will lead to peace.

(This article was first published in the *Open* magazine.)

REIMAGINING GOVERNANCE

This article was first published in April 2018 and comments on the transformative 115 Aspirational Districts Programme, a brainchild of Prime Minister Modi.

The 115 Aspirational Districts Programme conceived by Prime Minister Narendra Modi is radical not because this is the first time that a government in India has focussed on India's most backward districts, but because the exercise envisages a serious reimagination of government and governance, and deepens cooperative federalism. The programme is informed by the failures of the past and therefore has a more contemporary vision of how public services are best delivered to those who need them most.

Aspirational Districts

The 115 districts were chosen by senior officials of the Union government in consultation with state officials on the basis of a composite index of the following: deprivation enumerated under the Socio-Economic Caste Census, key health and education performance indicators, and the state of basic infrastructure. A minimum of one district was chosen from every state. Unsurprisingly, the largest concentration of districts is in the states which have historically under-performed such as Uttar Pradesh and Bihar, or which are afflicted by Left-wing extremism such as Jharkhand and Chhattisgarh. Moving forward, the areas that have been targeted for transformation are: education, health and nutrition, agriculture and water resources, financial inclusion, basic infrastructure and skills. Deliberately, the districts have been described as aspirational rather than backward so that they are viewed as islands of opportunity and hope rather than areas of distress and hopelessness. Attitudes and narrative matter for outcomes.

There is no financial package or large allocation of funds to this programme. The intent is to leverage the resources of the several government programmes that already exist but are not always used efficiently. The government doesn't always need to spend more to achieve outcomes, but instead to spend better. Many schemes of the Centre have flexible spending components which permit autonomy at the level of local governments but these are seldom used in practice due to controlling Central and state machineries.

Achieving success in this programme requires three tiers of government, the Centre, states and district administrations, to work in tandem. There is a structure in place. Each district is assigned a prabhari (in-charge) officer from the Centre (of Additional Secretary or Joint Secretary rank) and a prabhari officer from the state (of the rank of Secretary to state government) who will work in cooperation with the district administration. It is necessary for the Centre and states to be involved because not all decisions can be taken at the level of district. For example, if there is a shortage of teachers in a local school or a shortage of health personnel in a primary health centre, it needs the state capital to act, possibly through transfers of personnel from overstaffed areas. On financial inclusion, the full cooperation of banks is necessary and only the Central government has leverage over them. But most crucial is the District Magistrate or Collector who is familiar with the challenges of his or her geography and has considerable power to implement government schemes. Partnership is not something which comes easily to the upper tiers of government, which are used to dictating terms to lower tiers.

The spirit of cooperation needs to be supplemented by a culture of competition. This programme takes the principle of competitive federalism down to district administrations. Each district will be ranked on the focus areas which are disaggregated into easily quantifiable target areas. So as not to bias the rankings on historical achievements or lack of them, the rankings will be based on deltas or improvements, and are publicly available.

India's long history of a dominant State apparatus has led to an entrenched perception that government is the sole actor capable of and responsible for the transformation of India. The ADP has opened its door to civil society and leveraged the tool of corporate social responsibility to form partnerships which will bring new ideas and fresh energy with boots on the ground from non-government institutions to join the 'official' efforts. The force multiplier on outcomes from such participation is potentially massive.

Smart Data

One area which is being given serious attention is the collection of quality data on a real-time basis. Too often in India, data collection is delayed or lacking in quality which ends up leading to policymakers shooting in the dark. With continuously updated data dashboards, those running the programme on the ground can alter strategies after accurate feedback.

In a way, the ADP is a big pilot programme from reorienting how government does its business of delivering development. A decisive shift in the paradigm of governance is likely to finally fulfil the many broken promises of the past.

(This article was first published in *The Hindu*.)

MARKETS

INTRODUCTION: MARKETS

A strong case for free market economics has existed for almost two and a half centuries ever since Adam Smith wrote *An Inquiry into the Nature and Causes of the Wealth of Nations* in 1776. In the long period since then, economics has considerably evolved. It is well known that there are scenarios in which free markets may not produce optimal outcomes—in the case of public goods (defence, law and order), or merit goods (education, health) for example, or where there is asymmetry of information between market players or when there are significant economies of scale which lead to oligopolies and monopolies. There can be no such thing as a completely free market. The State needs to correct market failures.

Economic policy in post-Independent India followed the tradition of the erstwhile Soviet Union and Marxism socialism, which viewed markets with great suspicion. The State would occupy the commanding heights of the economy, and the private sector would be controlled by sundry mandarins. History shows us that every economy that has achieved sustained prosperity has done so by adopting a market economy with varying degrees of State intervention. When such intervention has been directed at addressing market failures, it has yielded positive results.

In India's political economy, free markets are associated with exclusion of the poor and perceived as being pro-rich. The reality is different. It was during the heydays of State intervention between 1947–1991 that India grew at a slow pace and was unable to lift hundreds of million out of poverty. That changed once India opened its doors to markets in 1991 and a record number came out of poverty over two decades of rapid growth. Perhaps the best example of how markets have led to inclusion of the marginalised is the telecom services sector.

Prior to liberalisation, when only the government operated telecom, a phone was a luxury in the possession only of the rich. Two and a half decades later, almost every Indian has access to a phone and some of the cheapest services anywhere in the world. That is the power of competitive markets in fostering inclusion.

The other key to well-functioning markets is competition, which also works as the best regulator of quality and prices. The State's role is to foster competition and not fix prices or production quantities via bureaucratic diktat. The State's role is also to focus on addressing market failures. These principles apply to agriculture, manufacturing and services, across the board, in every sector.

Markets have other, non-economic, upsides. In a democracy with several social cleavages, it often works to the advantage of political actors to perpetuate divides in a quest for votes. Therefore, the State, occupied by elected politicians, may not always act as leveller of society. On the other hand, impersonal market forces can act as a great leveller, bringing meritocracy to the forefront.

The essays in this section highlight the importance of markets in India's rise to prosperity and warn against the danger of inappropriate State intervention. Some of the chapters also elucidate the importance of social merit for markets in India.

THE IMPORTANCE OF BEING QAZI

This article was first published in October 2005, at a time when India's economy was in the midst of its very high growth phase of near double digits, the outcome of the market reforms undertaken by successive governments between 1991 and 2004. Many readers may not identify with Qazi Tauqeer, a Kashmiri youngster, who became a minor celebrity after he won a popular reality show on television. But his success story and that of many aspirational Indians owes much to economic liberalisation and the opportunities that markets present. On the contrary, governments haven't always created similar opportunities. In fact, governments may have denied many through explicit or implicit discrimination.

When Qazi Tauqeer was born in Srinagar, in 1986, India was different. Doordarshan was the single channel on television, Kashmir was at relative peace, and we were far from the 'shining' India that was to follow some years later, at least in some privileged places, for some privileged people. In 2005, Qazi Tauqeer, a singer and performer of some ability, became a TV celebrity, winner of Sony TV's Fame Gurukul, in an India with no less than seventy TV channels, a steadily increasing 'shine', and a much bruised, indeed battered, Kashmir. One could say Qazi has grown up through a period of huge change in Independent India.

The spread of markets with increasing opportunities for people and a deepening of political democracy are the upsides, while an increasing disillusionment with a sometimes arbitrary and seemingly corrupt State apparatus is the downside, most brutally exposed in Kashmir.

Markets have brought with them not only a huge range of goods, services and TV channels, but also a culture of individuality, opportunity and merit, quite distinct from the more parochial culture of caste, region and religion which ran and, in some places, still runs deep in India, especially in the functioning of institutions of the State. This is no surprise. The guardians of the State are only human. And humans are fallible, which makes the State fallible. It can be exploitative rather than helpful. This is not to argue that the State should not act at all. It should. But it must be a helpful, rather than cruel guardian. Qazi Tauqeer's success is good news for India and its people: its underlying secularism, quiet egalitarianism and democratic traditions.

A Kashmiri Muslim boy from a less than privileged background received no less than fifteen million votes from across India, saving him from eviction from the show ten times and finally perching him on the winners' podium with a lucrative singing contract and a brand new car as bonus. All that mattered to the voters was his ability—not his religion, not his place of birth, not his economic status. And the voters themselves, a staggering fifty million SMS messages received by the show, at last given a chance to elect someone on merit in a transparent fashion. This was quite unlike our general elections, where religion, region, caste, economic power and a lamentable absence of merit dominate the show. Indeed, barriers to entry are so formidable that the best do not even enter the contest. But lest we damn the State completely, its role in helping Taqueer reach where he did is crucial: the introduction of cable television in Kashmir in 1998 gave Qazi and many like him a connect to the world, and opportunities outside.

Is there an important lesson in Qazi's success for India's pressing problems? It is well known that India has no greater political problem than that of an estranged Kashmir. Perhaps instances like Qazi's win should help integrate more Kashmiri youth into the mainstream, rather than drive them to the path of violence. Perhaps the people of Kashmir will come around to see that the people of India at large harbour warmth and goodwill for them, whatever the State may stand for.

The achievements of Tauqeer, as well as others on television, may also show us the way forward in another pressing problem, that of missed economic opportunities. We need a move up the economic ladder as quickly as possible, for as many as possible. We need opportunities, equal and many.

We need merit. And we need the State to provide the basic minimum to all: not only food and clothing, but also shelter, healthcare and education, so that people are in a position to grasp the opportunities. We need the right mix of State and markets, sadly missing in India over the years, both in statist India and now in liberalised India. The churning must begin now, beginning with institutions of the State, and then, to fine tuning the role of markets in order to maximise benefits. Lest we forget, well done, Qazi Tauqeer. May you inspire many more to follow your path to hard-won success. And well done, people. Keep voting, preferably on merit. Keep yourselves empowered. You will get what you want, somewhere, and then, hopefully, everywhere.

(This article was first published in *The Indian Express*.)

IT ISN'T GAS: IF YOU FIX THE PRICE, YOU PAY A PRICE

This article was first published in February 2014 in the last months of the then UPA-II government led by Prime Minister Manmohan Singh. That government had been discredited by perceptions of rampant corruption and runaway inflation. This article argued that the gigantic twin failures of UPA-II, which would ultimately cost it dearly at the general election later that year, were because the fundamental tenets of sound economics had been brutally violated by the government, particularly the principle of letting the market rather than administrative fiat set prices.

The real problem is that the government has no business setting the price of gas or of any other commodity. But the Congress-led UPA had insisted on doing precisely that in a gamut of crucial sectors, be it gas, diesel, spectrum, coal mines, land and agriculture. It is this penchant for fixing prices by administrative fiat that had saddled the Congress and its allies with twin issues that cost them the general election: corruption and inflation.

Economics is an imprecise, dismal science. Still, it holds out some wisdom for the world. It tells us, for instance, that market mechanisms are far superior at discovering prices than bureaucrats or ministers are. Those who have defied this elementary truth have paid dearly: the erstwhile Soviet Union found itself bankrupt and quite literally broken after decades of price-fixing by sundry administrators. India too paid a heavy price for the government's dabbling in price-setting all the way up to 1991. If there was one thing liberalisation achieved, it was ridding us of the notion that bureaucrats knew best. Until that point, even steel prices were set by Delhi's Udyog Bhavan.

How ironic it is that the man who presided over the dismantling of several price controls in 1991, Dr Manmohan Singh, was the same man who presided over the fixing of so many prices some twenty years after liberalisation. It is his successors in the Congress, led by Rahul Gandhi, who now pay the price for fixing prices.

Take the case of gas. Almost a decade ago, in 2009, the UPA decided that Reliance would sell the gas from its KG Basin fields at the rate of 4.2 US dollars per unit. In 2013, it was decided that this price would be doubled to 8.4 per unit, to be effective from 1 April 2014. It was this doubling that Arvind Kejriwal (now, the chief minister of Delhi) was furious about. The point, however, was this: how could Kejriwal or anyone else know what was the right or wrong price? It is now commonly acknowledged by large numbers and including those who voted for the AAP that in Kejriwal's worldview, his administrative fiat is better than that of the Congress or BJP because he is not corrupt. Histrionics aside, that is hogwash.

For one, contrary to Kejriwal's claims back then in 2013–14, the UPA raised the price of gas based on a formula proposed by C. Rangarajan, the ex-Chairman of the Prime Minister's Council of Economic Advisors, and not on ministerial whim. But even then, as now, a bureaucrat is not the market. The right price of gas can only be determined by the forces of demand and supply, not just in India, but at a global level. Simply put, it means that any company selling gas firms up its price based on global factors—which change every hour, unlike bureaucratic decisions which tend to change every five years.

Sure, natural gas is a national resource and the government must get a share of its profits. The right way to do this is to charge royalties based on the market price of gas. There may be a case to subsidise end consumers (say, of power based on gas) when international market prices are high. Again, the way to address this is to target a subsidy at those consumers who need it, not control prices.

There are other ways to ensure that prices remain moderate. The best way is to ensure competition. Again, the way to do this is to encourage more private sector and foreign investors in the gas sector, something the government has been loath to do. And if a firm tries to overprice gas, there should be an independent regulatory mechanism, not the captive (to ministerial whim) Petroleum and Natural Gas Regulatory Board, which should play referee. The UPA had invested in none of these propositions. It fiddled with prices, waiting to be burned. Kejriwal certainly wasn't going to miss an opportunity.

It is incredible that the UPA did not learn its lesson on transparent pricing mechanisms despite the damage it incurred over its 2G spectrum allocations. It was in January 2008 that the then Telecom Minister, A. Raja overruled Prime Minister Manmohan Singh's request for an auction of 2G spectrum and doled out 122 licences based on a whimsical version of a first-come-first-serve policy, whimsical because procedures were manipulated at the last minute to ensure than even the first-come-first-served principle was brutally violated.

Even in the 2G scam, it is important to distinguish the

conspiracy from the arbitrary fixing of prices. The conspiracy involved procedural violations and money trails that suggested a quid pro quo. The fixing of the licence fee at a rate determined fit by the government is not a conspiracy in itself. It is just old-fashioned socialist planning of the bureaucrat-knows-best kind.

Much was made of the report of the Comptroller and Auditor General (CAG), which in 2010 declared that the exchequer may have incurred a loss of up to 1.76 lakh crores by not auctioning 2G spectrum. Some were outraged at Raja. He lost his job. Others were outraged at the CAG; how on earth had he calculated such a huge figure? The truth is that the CAG, like Raja, would have no precise idea on the right price of spectrum. Only a free, competitive market can discover that price, not a bureaucracy, not an accountant. But the UPA had only itself to blame for facing the brunt of the CAG's report. If it had reposed its faith in the market pricing mechanism, there would have been no scandal.

Incredibly, exactly the same thing was permitted in the allocation of coal mines in 2009, several months after the 2G scam had already raised its ugly head in media reports. Once again, liberalisation's father, Manmohan Singh initially asked for auctions in the allocation of these mines, only to back off in favour of administrative allotments. Again, giving out coal mines free may or may not point to corruption. The government may deliberately have wanted to provide cheap inputs to power-producing companies. But in an atmosphere where the government is distrusted and crony capitalism is rampant, it is a folly to rely on an administrative rather than free-market mechanism for such an allocation of resources. Again, it is impossible to say whether the CAG was right in estimating the losses from Coalgate at 1.8 lakh crore rupees. A free market mechanism may not have yielded the same figure had the mines been openly auctioned. But the UPA had only itself to blame for subverting the market.

Together, Coalgate and 2G destroyed the UPA's credibility. They led to an unprecedented policy paralysis, which crippled the economy and saw economic growth fall from 8.5 to 4.5 per cent in a period of three years. It gave the Opposition plenty of fodder to attack the UPA on corruption and its economic record. It gave Kejriwal the opportunity to attack the UPA on Reliance and gas pricing just two months before the general election. And all of that because the UPA forgot that one golden rule of economics: let prices be determined by demand and supply.

If corruption—or at least perceptions of it—was the UPA's black stain, then inflation (very real, no perception) was its Achilles heel. The unabated price rise of UPA's second term in office can directly be traced to food items, particularly vegetables, fruits, milks and protein that are produced by the country's vast agriculture sector. The UPA put forward a simple explanation for the persistent, usually double-digit rate of food inflation. It said that inflation was the price being paid for prosperity as a rise in incomes (particularly rural incomes courtesy the UPA's welfare programmes) had outstripped the supply of agricultural commodities. In this explanation, the UPA was apparently embracing conventional economics: prices rise when demand exceeds supply.

Unfortunately, the UPA was peddling a half-truth. It said nothing about the supply side, even though it spent a lot of time and money fiddling with the market mechanism (particularly prices), which ultimately determines that supply.

The UPA's favourite instrument in agriculture was the Minimum Support Price (MSP), a floor price the government offers rice and wheat farmers to procure their produce. The aim of the MSP is noble, to guarantee farmers a good price, but its side effects are devastating. First, the MSP is unidirectional; year after year, it is only raised, not reduced even in times of a bumper crop. This affects inflationary expectations in the rest of the economy. Second, since the MSP is available only to producers of cereals, there is a perverse incentive for all farmers to grow rice and wheat at the expense of fruits and vegetables, which do not have any guaranteed price and are prone to high rates of damage. This creates a supply shortage in precisely those commodities that are growing fastest in demand (demand for cereals tends to grow much slower compared to vegetables and proteins as incomes rise). The fact is that the government's MSP policy fuelled food inflation.

Unfortunately, the government's price intervention in agriculture did not end with the MSP. The UPA, more than any other government, used export bans of key agricultural commodities (such as onions and cotton) in desperate attempts to control domestic prices. These have been counter-productive. It kills the incentive for a farmer to produce more of a commodity if he is denied its global best price. This creates a vicious cycle of shortages. Ideally, the government ought to have loosened imports at times of shortage, but the mandarins of the UPA were addicted to playing havoc with proper price signals. It's for the same reason that the temptation to ban futures trading in agricultural goods surfaces from time to time. All that a ban does is deny farmers a useful market price signal and the agricultural economy an automatic correction mechanism. If prices are high today, farmers will produce more, forcing prices down in the future. This is elementary economics, but it was totally lost on the UPA.

(This article was first published in the *Open* magazine.)

DOES INDIA REALLY WANT 10% GROWTH?

This article was written in 2015 when Prime Minister Modi was still relatively new in office. Events since then have only reinforced how India's political economy remains reined against free markets in critical sectors like land, labour and capital. Modi hasn't succeeded in pushing through the reforms necessary for double-digit growth, pushed back by the political blowback of being labelled a 'suit-boot ki sarkar'. That doesn't make these reforms any less necessary. A winning political argument is awaited.*

For rapid growth, the nation needs to shake off the false narratives of the past, and embrace liberalisation and reforms.

Double-digit growth is more than an impressive statistic. It is the surest path to prosperity. China has shown us that. So have South Korea, Taiwan, and Singapore. The question is why India has found it so difficult to break the ten per cent barrier. The answer is that India's political economy has not been ready to create the policy environment for rapid growth. This is not the equivalent of saying democracies cannot achieve what

* A reference made by Rahul Gandhi against Prime Minister Modi's government, alluding to its pro-rich policies.

authoritarian or semi-authoritarian regimes can. Democracies can, as long as the political leadership builds a convincing case for double-digit growth and the people accept that vision.

India's political economy has always been shy to admit the most obvious impact of double-digit growth—people are going to become rich, admittedly in very varying degrees. India's long legacy of socialism has consequences not just in terms of the policy regime, but also in terms of the dominant narrative in politics. While many of the worst aspects of socialism have been gradually dismantled in the policy sphere over the last two decades, the political economy has stuck to the ancient regime, something that was exemplified by the protests against a mildly reformist land acquisition bill.

If India is to achieve ten per cent growth, the political economy needs to rid itself of *faux* socialism. India needs someone to change the narrative of political economy and for the people of India to accept it. Prime Minister Narendra Modi, unburdened by the legacy of Nehruvian socialism and gifted with an impressive majority, is perfectly positioned to make the case.

He needs to strengthen his case by making the argument for liberalising the three most crucial markets in any economy—those for land, labour, and capital. The fracas over the government's proposed amendments to the land acquisition bill is the perfect opportunity to make the reformist case. It is plainly absurd to suggest that the land acquisition bill is anti-farmer. Behind that argument, made by assorted Left-of-Centre politicians, is the belief that farmers must be confined to what in India is low-productivity farming, through which a majority of the people employed in agriculture barely make a living. India cannot become prosperous if fifty per cent of its workforce remains in agriculture, a sector that produces only fifteen per cent of its GDP.

Why should we assume that farmers do not want to sell their land—for a good price of course—and move to more rewarding occupations? In fact, a brave politician would argue for the elimination of any specific law on acquiring land. Like any other goods or service, the sale and purchase of land should be determined by the market. Logically, there has to be some price at which farmers will sell and industry will buy. Why should the government pre-determine it at four times the 'market price?' It could be more in cases. It could be less in others. That is the kind of radical thinking that enables double-digit growth. Given the circumstances, for now, the prime minister must stick to his stand on the changes to the land bill and eliminate unnecessary bureaucratic procedures that slow down the process of acquiring land and make it more expensive.

The mythical narratives on land acquisition are matched by the blatantly false narratives on labour. India's existing labour laws don't hamper industry alone. They harm the cause of labour itself. Consider this telling statistic: the proportion of India's workforce in the informal sector (not governed by labour laws) is around ninety per cent. Shockingly, that is roughly the same proportion as in 1991, when economic reforms began. If India has to boost its manufacturing base—the key to double-digit growth—it must liberalise its labour laws. The fact is that while this will benefit entrepreneurs, it will equally benefit workers, many more of whom will find jobs in the formal sector, which promises greater security and benefits. The bogey of 'hire and fire' has been used for years to block labour law reform. The only people who benefit from no hire and fire are the small proportion of workers who are engaged in the formal labour force at present and whose productivity is low because they have no incentive to perform. Modi needs to persuade India that market reform in labour is pro-growth and pro-labour.

The market for capital has arguably seen greater reform than land and labour. However, it has not been reformed enough to benefit small entrepreneurs and ordinary consumers. The system works for big businesses, which are able to borrow at reasonable rates from both banks and capital markets. But small businesses and ordinary consumers are either locked out or have to borrow at expensive rates. Further liberalisation of the banking system in particular, which will increase competition, will benefit growth and be in the interest of those excluded from the system. Liberalisation is good for the excluded as much as for the privileged. But few make this argument convincingly to India's wider political economy. Needless to say, India's political economy will still demand certain things from the State. The reform of the institutions of State—whether in law and order, education, health or sanitation—is a critical component of achieving double-digit growth. A better functioning State machinery will also make people more receptive to market-based reform. A corrupt and inept State machinery only makes people believe that market reform is a smokescreen for crony capitalism. And it is true that crony capitalism has made it harder for political leaders to make the case for rules-based capitalism. The stark reality is that India can achieve double-digit growth only with rules-based capitalism and an efficient State machinery. India must decide whether it wants that system badly enough. It is, after all, much easier to retain the status quo and grow at a sub-ten per cent rate. That though isn't enough for aspirational India.

(This article was first published in *The Sunday Guardian.*)

WHY IT ISN'T WRONG TO BE RIGHT

This article was first published in December 2013 as the campaign for the 2014 general election was underway. One of the choices before voters was to elect either the Centre-Left Congress-led coalition with its emphasis on a big role for the government and redistribution, or the Centre-Right BJP led by Narendra Modi campaigning on a minimum government, maximum governance platform. This article makes the case for mainstreaming Centre-Right thinking in India, and not treating it is as a 'pro-rich' or elitist fringe.

In India's mainstream thinking, it is almost taboo to carry the label of Right-wing. It usually conjures up images of Trishul-wielding fanatics who are out to penalise minorities, or more accurately anyone who disagrees with their view of the world. Now, every label has its fringe. The extreme Right, usually wedded to some form of cultural nationalism or brute majoritarian instincts, has been a destructive force in history. But then so has the extreme-Left. Adolf Hitler committed unspeakable crimes in the name of Right-wing politics, just as Joseph Stalin murdered millions of innocent people in the name of Left-wing politics. Fortunately, in democracies like India, there is very little room for either extreme—the loony fringe is also the isolated fringe. Pluralistic societies inevitably pull politics to the Centre. There is, however, room to lean either Left or Right while standing at the Centre.

A Centre-Right vision of India's future gives primacy to market forces (rather than the State) in determining the country's economic future. It does not preclude cultural liberalism. In fact, the health of free market economy depends on the freedom of its participants, unencumbered by cultural conservatism of any kind.

India has long been dominated by forces of the Centre-Left. In the economic sphere, the mixed-up policies of Congress-style socialism have resulted in sluggish growth, inflationary spells and continuous poverty. Countries that were far poorer than India in 1950 (Korea, Malaysia, Thailand) are now much richer, because they relied more heavily on market forces. After ten years of uninterrupted rule by the populist, Centre-Left, Congress and its allies which pushed our economy into the doldrums, a Centre-Right economic agenda seems like the only alternative. India stands on the cusp (of either sinking into stagnation, or rising from the dead) just as advanced economies like the US and UK did in the late 1970s. The rise of Ronald Reagan and Margaret Thatcher was at least partly due to the dramatic failure of the Centre-Left in the decade that preceded their arrival.

In the Indian context, there are other advantages to unleashing a market economy. Several old divisions—whether based on religion, caste, region or language—are reinforced by the polity and the State. The bogey of reservations, based on some historical divisions in society, is the basic instinct of almost every political party. Markets, which give preference to merit than accidents of birth can paper over these cleavages. Markets can be a stronger force for more liberalism and tolerance in society than any political party can ever be.

Is there a role for the State in this Centre-Right vision of

India? Yes, there is. The State needs to be a referee. It needs to be an effective regulator of market forces so that excesses of the kind which we saw before the onset of the global financial crisis of 2008 are curbed. In India, the State must also play a role in financing the building of infrastructure; physical infrastructure like roads, ports and irrigation; social infrastructure like education and health. But financing is not the same as delivery. In India, the government has been a poor deliverer of public services. There is, therefore, a case to be made for public financing combined with private deliver.

The State must ensure that everyone has the basic necessities they need to participate in the market—dole is never the answer, productive investment in human capabilities is.

An efficient market, which is be populated by skilled individuals (who have all constitutionally guaranteed rights) is India's only path to economic prosperity, and modern society. That's a Centre-Right vision. And it isn't wrong.

(This article was first published in *Firstpost.com*)

STATE VS. MARKET: GROW UP

This article was first published in October 2009 soon after the announcement of the Nobel Prize in Economics for Elinor Ostrom and Oliver Williamson. The article examines the importance of their work in the centuries-old State versus market debate in economics. Ultimately, it is important to recognise that the dichotomies often presented between the State and market are not useful. For prosperity, an economy needs both, provided they are playing the right roles.

The Nobel Prize for Economics is, of course, primarily about honouring outstanding researchers and their contribution to the discipline. But very often, circumstances of the real world embedded in economics influence the decision of who wins at what point in time. Paul Krugman's win in 2008 was in equal measure recognition of his original research in trade theory as well as his general scepticism of the efficiency of free markets. The prize was handed out when free markets were going through their roughest patch in decades. Similarly, George Akerlof, Michael Spence and Joseph Stiglitz who worked on market failure because of asymmetric information shared the prize in 2001, the year after the spectacular burst of the dotcom bubble. Prof. Amartya Sen had earlier won in 1998 for welfare economics (he is also a known free market sceptic), the year after the East Asian crisis and in the aftermath of the crises in Russia and Brazil.

It was quite a trend every time free market capitalism went through a crisis anywhere, the Nobel Committee chose to award economists who had made their academic reputations questioning the efficacy of the free market.

In 2009, there came a surprise. The winners were Elinor Ostrom, the first woman to win a Nobel in Economics was ironically a professor of Political Science, and Oliver Williamson a student and long-time collaborator of Ronald Coase, a previous winner of the prize (in 1991). They were cited for their work on economic governance: Ostrom for her study of the management of common resources, and Williamson for his study of the firm as an institution for conflict resolution.

At a time when the world was still obsessively debating the merits of free markets, and the appropriate balance between the State and markets, the 2009 prize recognised the work of researchers who highlighted the importance of using economics to understand and analyse institutions beyond the market (and the State). This is of critical importance because we (economists in particular) often forget that important economic activity often takes place outside the strict boundaries of the market and State. The firm is one such institution. Also, many transactions can actually be efficiently completed without the involvement of either the market or the State.

In fact, Ostrom's empirical research on the common use of resources like lakes, woods and fish stocks showed that outcomes are often better when users manage these common resources as they exist, and not when compared with a situation when the same resources are privatised or regulated by the State. In that sense her empirical work challenged mainstream disposition in favour of privatising resources (including common resources) for their efficient use. Her work is relevant even today in India as we continue to grapple with how best to manage and indeed use depleting natural resources—forests, fish stocks and minerals, for example, which groups of people (particularly tribals) view as commonly owned. Private acquisition of these resources has met with much resistance, just as State regulation hasn't worked as an alternative, without provoking conflict. Perhaps it's time we considered alternate ways outside the rather strictly demarcated and strongly contested private control or State control conceptions about the use of common resources.

The work of Oliver Williamson is in the tradition of Ronald Coase's work on the theory of the firm. Willamson's work emphasises the point that when competition is limited, as it often is in the real world (as opposed to the conventional perfect competition assumption), firms with hierarchical structures are better institutions of conflict resolution than markets are.

At first observation, the work of both Olstrom and Williamson suggest instinctive scepticism of free markets. That may have something to do with the empirical nature of their work. It is easier to build efficient markets on the drawing board than to find them operating in the real world. Market imperfections are a fact of life, and it is good to see the normally theory-leaning Nobel Committee rewarding empirical research in economics.

But what differentiated Olstrom and Williamson from other market sceptics is that they didn't, by default, fall to the State as the best alternative institution. Perhaps, amidst all the furious, but completely binary State vs market debate surrounding the economics/economic policy debate, the Nobel Committee just sent a gentle reminder that economics is a much bigger, broader and more credible discipline than recent public perception has unfortunately come to view it.

(This article was first published in the *Financial Express.*)

POVERTY OF SOCIALISM

This article was first published in December 2011 at a time when the then UPA-II government was sliding into a state of policy paralysis following poor economic management and questionable decision-making. This article makes the argument that governments which try and interfere too much in the functioning of markets are doomed to fail. It explains the reasons why UPA-II paid a heavy political price in 2014. The lessons are applicable for any government which follows a similar anti-market path.

Governments that meddle in markets rarely deliver prosperity. They redistribute poverty instead. The Congress-led coalition was no different. Its two flagship legislations, the Food Security Act and the National Rural Employment Guarantee Act (NREGA), wreaked havoc on two crucial markets: the market for food and the market for jobs. The genuinely urgent goals of alleviating hunger and providing gainful employment were thus set back by decades.

The food security legislation makes it mandatory for the government to sell highly subsidised rice, wheat and coarse grain to 63.5 per cent of India's population through government-owned fair price shops. The first distortion of incentives takes place at the fair price shop. The owners of these shops see the obvious opportunity for price arbitrage. The government procures wheat at twelve rupees per kg from farmers, but sells it at two rupees per kg through fair price shops. A dishonest shop owner makes a killing by selling the government-supplied wheat in the open market at a price between two rupees and the open market price. The latter is bound to be higher than the government-set cost price of twelve rupees per kg. After the diversion, the poor only get access to a limited amount of the worst quality cereals that remain unsold. The open market provides no succour. The prices there are higher than they were before the food security legislation. To meet its legal obligation, the government has to purchase at least fifty per cent of the total cereal production. That restricts supply to the open market and sends prices soaring. It costs 96,000 crores a year (nineteen billion US dollars) to hurt the poor like this. The government could spend the same amount investing in irrigation, in rural roads, and in supply chain infrastructure like storage. That kind of intervention would not distort markets. It would, however, boost output and productivity and ensure that Indian farmers, also India's poorest, can feed themselves without government support.

The National Rural Employment Guarantee Act makes it legally mandatory for the government to provide a hundred days of employment every year to one member of every rural household. The approximate wage for a day's work is a hundred rupees. Annual income from the programme for an individual is 10,000 rupees. By another calculation, it is thirty rupees per day, below the poverty line of thirty-two rupees per capita per day defined by the Planning Commission. It costs 40,000 crore rupees a year (eight billion US dollars) to keep the beneficiaries of the programme under the national poverty line. The collateral damage is larger. The rural employment guarantee programme pushes up minimum wages, deterring potential employers from hiring cheap labour. Those looking for a proper 365-day job lose out to the hundred-day beneficiaries.

The government could easily spend 40,000 crores a year educating Indians. That would not distort the labour market while making people eminently qualified to get a proper job. It is one of India's great ironies that industry and even agriculture, prefer to employ relatively expensive capital rather than relatively cheap labour. The formal organised sector of the economy only employs seven per cent of the workforce. That percentage is unchanged since 1991. But no government has bothered to reform India's archaic labour laws which disallow hire-and-fire, sending ninety-three per cent of the workforce into the relative poverty of informal employment.

(This article was first published in *The Sunday Guardian*.)

TIME'S UP FOR SOCIALIST HANGOVER

This article was first published in 2015 when the Modi government was less than a year into its term. Since then, the government has taken some strides in closing down sick public sector companies: around twenty are undergoing closure. It has also restarted the long-stalled strategic disinvestment or privatisation programme. Around forty public sector companies, including Air India, have been approved in principle for strategic disinvestment. Nothing symbolises the sloth and inefficiency of India's tryst with socialism than public sector enterprises. Downsizing the public sector is a work in progress.

The news of the imminent closure of HMT Watches in 2014 was startling for two reasons. It was a big surprise to learn that the firm was still running and producing watches. It was almost shocking to learn that the government was apparently being bold enough to shut down a public sector company. A majority of middle-class Indians of a certain vintage would have owned an HMT watch, just as they would have likely owned a Premier Padmini or Ambassador car—coincidentally the latter shut down production in May 2016. It is unlikely however that either HMT or Ambassador would have been the choice of anyone in middle class India in the last twenty-five years.

For HMT, it showed in the numbers. The company recorded

losses for fifteen consecutive years between 1999 and 2014. There was no way an antiquated, slow-moving public sector company was going to ever compete with nimble private sector players, whether domestic or foreign.

HMT didn't even have the luxury of massive government procurement, something that kept Ambassador alive until 2016. That car, based on a 1950s technology and design, and produced in the private sector died a natural death once it became clear that government departments and agencies would now buy other more modern and more economical cars.

In different ways, both HMT Watches and Ambassador are prime examples of all that was wrong with socialist India and how the hangover continues to linger. The Ambassador was proof of how a government-protected private sector thrived at the expense of consumer interest. It laid the foundation of crony capitalism. HMT Watches was an example of how the State got its priorities badly wrong. Should the government have ever bothered manufacturing relatively low-technology consumer goods like watches, when its priority ought to have been to produce enough literate Indians who would have the capacity to read the time?

The failure of the socialist State to provide universal education and healthcare of a reasonable quality has had greater adverse consequences for India than its failure to produce watches profitably. And yet, twenty-seven years after liberalisation, the government continues to be obsessed about running public sector companies in completely unnecessary domains (in these areas, the private sector already does a good job of providing quality services at competitive prices) like aviation, hospitality (ITDC) and telecom (VSNL, MTNL). If only the government showed equal vigour and determination (with a greater efficiency of course) in running primary education or primary healthcare. The private sector can't be a perfect substitute in these sectors.

Might the closing down of HMT Watches signal a change? It is hard to be optimistic. Unlike Air India, MTNL and ITDC, HMT Watches is a small company with just 1,000 employees. Its cumulative losses over fifteen years are 1,500 crores. Air India received twenty times that amount as a bailout in 2015. Also, let's face it, the power of patronage in a watch-manufacturer is far less than in an airline, or a hotel business, or a telecom empire. There is a great incentive for politicians to keep those companies going.

Still, one must hope. If the Ambassador car and HMT Watches have shut shop, India may yet overcome its socialist hangover some day in the not-so-distant future.

(This article was first published in *The Sunday Guardian.*)

'UNPOPULIST' NEED NOT BE UNPOPULAR

This article was first published in 2014 a few months after the Modi government assumed office. The economy was in poor shape with slow growth and high inflation, in desperate need of tough decisions to set it on the right path. One view of India's political economy is that it is impossible for politicians to eschew populism which usually under-prices key services and goods, ultimately damaging government finances and sound macroeconomic management. Populism is always value destroying. A prosperous market economy needs a stable macroeconomic environment of low government deficits and moderate inflation. The Modi government has decisively reined in careless government expenditure and kept a lid on inflation, abandoning the commonly implemented strategy of boosting growth marginally by letting inflation go out of control. It has won several state elections subsequently. But the final test will be in 2018–19 culminating in the general election. Will the government remain 'unpopulist' and popular? Modi's experience in Gujarat would suggest it is possible.

Is an 'unpopulist' policy decision the same as an 'unpopular' decision? The government's move to hike railway fares by almost fifteen per cent at one go in 2014 was the first step in reversing the careless populism of the UPA. But did it dent the popularity of Narendra Modi's government? In a country grappling with high inflation and stagnant growth (and flat incomes, limited job opportunities), any rise in prices isn't exactly good news. However, a hike in rail fares turned out to be popular, because it was accompanied by a promise of radical improvement in the quality of services delivered by the railways.

It is plain wrong to assume that all Indian consumers care about is the price of a good or service. Quality matters. People will pay a higher fare happily if they can get a reservation at short notice, or if they can access clean toilets on trains, or if they can wait at clean, air-conditioned stations. The allegedly populist Indian citizen has shown the appetite to pay elsewhere, for example, to pay more for electricity, provided that there is quality 24x7 supply. There is no use paying a 'populist' rate and getting no power or very limited power. For water too, people will pay, provided they are assured quality supply all day and all week long. Narendra Modi knows this from his experience in Gujarat.

Modi's government at the Centre will need to take many more 'unpopulist' decisions in order to get the economy back on track. It needs to, therefore, communicate aggressively and effectively that while Indians may have to pay more for some government services, they will be compensated by the highest quality in the delivery of those services. It hasn't quite done that in the context of the railway fare hike, choosing to 'blame' its predecessor government for the decision. That's a strategy with severe limits—voters will soon forget the UPA's tenure and begin to hold the NDA accountable for all that's wrong.

The challenge is that while user charges, whether for railways, water, power or universities can be hiked by administrative fiat in one stroke of a pen, it will take a lot longer, possibly a time period measured in years rather than days or months, to upgrade the quality of services provided by the railways or power utilities, or even universities. Modi needs people to have faith in his policies—that they will show results in the long run.

In Gujarat, Narendra Modi proved that good economics can also be good politics as long as the government is efficient. Good economics and good politics come into conflict only when the government fails to play its proper role. The Modi government has to be decisive in the seemingly intractable interaction between economic wisdom and political outcomes.

(This article was first published in *The Sunday Guardian.*)

SLUMDOG ENTREPRENEURS

This article was first published in January 2009 at a time when the English language movie, Slumdog Millionaire, was winning accolades around the world. The article contextualises the film in the emergence of a market economy in India post 1991. Contrary to what many critics said was a depiction of India's dirty underbelly, the argument in this piece is that, in fact, the story reflects the rise of a new India, hardly rich but full of enterprise. Outside the story, the rise of a globally competitive Indian film industry by the late 2000s is also a reflection of the power of markets.

Almost a decade ago in 2008, the success of *Slumdog Millionaire* at award nights and box offices overseas brought much joy to the public at large in India. After all, it had been a long time since a movie filmed in India, and set entirely around an Indian story bagged so much attention in the West. The last film to do something similar was Richard Attenborough's multiple Oscar winning *Gandhi*, released in 1982. Like *Slumdog*, it was produced and directed by 'foreigners', but it was a story about India, filmed in India.

Slumdog had provoked reactions beyond the artistic merits or faults of the film. Amitabh Bachchan was hardly the only Indian who felt strongly about the film depicting the dirty underbelly of a Third World nation to Western audiences who would lap it up. After all, India's image in the world had undergone great transformation from just a dirty poor nation full of slums and deprivation, to a potential economic and (to a lesser extent) political powerhouse.

Back in the early 1980s, though, when *Gandhi* became one of the most critically acclaimed movies of its time, we were indeed a different India, an India accustomed more to the moribund Hindu rate of growth (three–four per cent) than aspirations to match the world's best in any sphere, whether in building globally competitive business or in making world class films. At that time, our best brand abroad was probably Mahatma Gandhi, and the non-violent movement for Independence that he had led three decades earlier. The West was more captivated by what the freedom movement had achieved, than by the things India had achieved after Independence with our closed, statist, slow-growing economy, and our ill-fated tilt towards the erstwhile Soviet Union.

However, economic reforms started changing the way India viewed itself. They were also the reason that changed the way the West viewed India. Over the last four decades and more, we have opened up our economy, and registered growth rates of up to nine per cent. In the process, we have created world class companies in IT, pharma, automobiles and beyond. We now successfully compete with global leaders in global markets. We have created more billionaires than in China. So why—the sceptics ask in their first grievance with *Slumdog*—isn't Western-made cinema choosing to depict this face of India. After all, most mainstream Indian films in early 2000s, like, Karan Johar's *Kabhie Khushi Kabhie Gham,* did succeed in showcasing a prosperous and glamorous side of India. In fact, until the end of the 1980s, Amitabh Bachchan himself had made the role of the frustrated (sans any glamour) angry young man, all his own. But if Indian films changed their perception about India, why weren't films made in the West about India doing the same, asked critics.

A second possible grievance was: as was proven in early 2000, when Indian filmmakers were matching world-class standards in producing films, and had moved on from what some may consider as poorly-produced movies of the 1970s and 1980s, why should a Western-made film about India gather so much attention? In fact, the indigenous film industry in India was the only film industry (along with Hong Kong) which held out and beat down competition from Hollywood, something which the once mighty, and still haughty, continental European film industry failed to do.

The unique formula of made-in-India films (which deems almost every movie to be a colourful musical, and or a great Indian family saga) has helped corner a big market in India and a growing market of NRIs (and other expats from South Asia) overseas. And let's face it: it's big money. The Indian film industry should not worry about Western appreciation or winning an Oscar. It should just focus on remaining competitive.

The first depiction of underbelly grievance isn't particularly important or relevant either. It's true that *Slumdog,* or indeed the Man Booker Prize winning novel, *White Tiger* by Aravind Adiga in 2008 depicted the underbelly of India and garnered attention because of the subject matter. But let's be honest and admit that we still have a dirty underbelly. After all, India still has the largest number of poor people in the world.

However, the more fascinating aspect of the stories of both *Slumdog* and *White Tiger* was missed in the general discourse. Interestingly, both stories featured as their central character, someone dirt poor who, through the effort of enterprise (legitimate, illegitimate, or plain luck), becomes rich. Neither story was about the hopelessness of poverty—instead, they were about the aspirations and real possibilities of escaping that poverty. That, in a sense, depicted the new India. Of course we have our world class companies, films and billionaires. But we also have millions of other less known entrepreneurs who are finding opportunities to climb the economic ladder. They are increasingly, and positively, choosing not to accept their poverty like earlier generations may have.

So while the Indian film industry depicts the affluent face of the new India, somebody also needs to depict the not-so-affluent, but equally aspirational and ambitious side of the other India. The West, and indeed India, need to understand the co-existence of these two worlds, which are two generations away from Gandhi, one generation away from economic stagnation, and a generation here to seize their moment, with generous helpings of enterprise and hard work and some amount of bending the rules. Like it or not, that's the real India.

(This article was first published in the *Financial Express*.)

RELIANCE ON COMPETITION

This article was first published in May 2010 just after a truce was signed by the warring Ambani brothers, Mukesh and Anil. Perhaps no company more than Reliance is more symbolic of the best of Indian capitalism as well as its flaws. The central argument in this article is valid eight years later: that Indian entrepreneurs are better advised to spend their considerable creative energies in competing with each other in a competitive market rather than trying to engage in rent-seeking or other kinds of value-destroying acts. That is what will bring real legitimacy to capitalism in India which is so often undermined by reckless crony capitalism.

The late Dhirubhai Ambani may have been a controversial figure to many shades of opinion during his lifetime, but let's face it, he was the first Indian entrepreneur who truly believed that an Indian company could be world class and globally competitive. Almost every entrepreneur of his vintage had to be able to play the licence raj. The complexity and ridiculousness of rules and regulations made it impossible to do business in a normal fashion. But while other entrepreneurs were satisfied with playing the system and then simply hiding behind the protection offered by government policies, Dhirubhai Ambani had greater ambition. And so, while many inefficient entrepreneurs of his vintage simply faded away after liberalisation in 1991, Reliance only grew in strength. Dhirubhai was also the first entrepreneur who genuinely wanted to create wealth for a larger number of people than just his own family. Unsurprisingly he was the father of the equity cult in India at a time when stock markets had few takers.

That is the essence of the legacy that was inherited by Mukesh and Anil Ambani after Dhirubhai's death in 2002. But the constant warring between the brothers, in the run-up to their formal split in 2006, and thereafter, has taken a toll on that legacy. The split up of the empire took an obvious toll on unified Reliance's status, but the distractions of the personal battle between the two brothers would have shifted some of the focus away from making each of the two new companies world beaters in their own right. Needless to say, the feuding, particularly the high-profile battle over gas from the KG basin imposed a heavy price on shareholders of both companies—the kind of value destruction that Dhirubhai is unlikely to have tolerated.

Viewed in this context, the signing of a truce between Mukesh and Anil Ambani in May 2010 was a significant step in the restoration of the original Ambani legacy. It was actually much more than that, with impact on government policy, investment climate, stock markets and the Indian economy at large.

The centrepiece of the truce between the two brothers was an agreement to annul all the 'non-compete' agreements signed by RIL and Reliance-ADAG at the time of their split in 2006. Now, both companies are free to operate in what until now was the other's exclusive domain. There is one exception though:

gas-based power generation will remain the domain of Anil Ambani's ADAG until 2022. But otherwise, for example, RIL has stormed into telecom, financial services are open for them and power while Reliance-ADAG can enter the oil and gas and petrochemicals segment. Also, importantly, neither company can block the other's investment plans by citing the right of first refusal agreement between the two.

At one level, it almost sounds ironic that there was ever a 'non-compete' agreement between the two companies given the bitter rivalry and 'competition' that was on display. In effect, what the non-compete agreements restricted was any competition in the free market. What they did not restrict was competition on the exact terms and interpretation of the non-compete agreements. Those have been fought out in the corridors of the government policy establishment and in the courts. And we know very well from the long history of business in India, and indeed elsewhere, that when competition plays out in corridors or chambers rather than the marketplace, outcomes are hardly optimal. In Dhirubhai's era, there was perhaps no other way, but almost twenty years after liberalisation, the market is where all corporate battles ought to play out.

The most public, high-profile and damaging of all the differences between the companies was, of course, over supply of gas from RIL's Krishna–Godavari basin bloc to RNRL's gas-based power plants. The root of the dispute lay in a private MoU apparently signed at the time of separation in 2006. That MoU promised Anil Ambani's RNRL a supply of gas from RIL at almost half the rate of the government determined price. RIL later refused to sell gas at below the government-determined price. The government supported RIL's position. RNRL, of course, refused to accept either RIL's or the government's position. Plenty of accusations flew from all sides and the case went to the Supreme Court. The SC finally ruled in favour of RIL and the government, and that put the matter to rest. But not without considerable collateral damage in the interim.

The stocks of both companies went through long periods of ups and downs. Given that the market capitalisation of the two groups is some ten per cent of the total market capitalisation of BSE and NSE, what happens to the stock of these two companies matters to the health of the market overall. Neither company did service to its own shareholders or other participants in the stock market through their dispute.

The collateral damage from the warring brothers went beyond the market. The entire dispute over gas cast a serious shadow on the credibility of government policy in this crucial area. Gas is going to be an increasingly important and clean source of energy in the years to come. A transparent and credible atmosphere is critical to attract the kind of investment that is necessary to exploit the potential of gas fully. The Ministry of Petroleum and Natural Gas has had only limited success in previous auctions for exploration and licensing. The continuation of the Reliance dispute for a long period of time only made prospective investors more nervous.

Now, with the SC decision and truce between the Ambani brothers, there is a window of opportunity to clear the murk in the gas sector. The successful conclusion of the renegotiation of gas price between RIL and RNRL ordered by the SC showed the way for the 'cooperation' and 'collaboration' promised by the brothers.

The plain fact of the matter is that the Ambani brothers are too gifted a set of entrepreneurs to fritter away their energies targeting each other, or unnecessarily cranking the levers of government. Their considerable energies and talent would be better spent building the business empires they each own. If not for the country, they should do so for Dhirubhai.

(This article was first published in *The Indian Express*.)

BHARAT, INDIA AND A THIRD INDIA: THE IMPORTANCE OF THE NOT-RICH, NOT-POOR

This article was first published in April 2014, one month before Narendra Modi won a clear mandate from the people of India. This article argues that since the economic liberalisation of 1991 and the ushering of a market economy, the old duality between the rich (usually in big cities) and the poor (mostly in the villages) has made for a new order where a clear majority of Indians are not the rich in big cities or the poor in villages, but a third set of aspirational Indians who live in smaller towns and larger rural habitations. It is this class that saw upward mobility post-liberalisation. At the same time, the market economy has made this class highly aspirational and demanding from the political leadership. Whoever wants to win the mandate in 2019 needs to win over this section of voters.

Come 2019, Narendra Modi wants their vote. So do Rahul Gandhi and Arvind Kejriwal. They are the seventy crore (700 million) Indians who are neither desperately poor, nor comfortably middle class. Modi calls them the neo-middle class. Rahul calls them the working class. Kejriwal would probably call them the *aam aadmis* (the common people).

The fact is that as a composite group, they are larger in number than the poor (300 million) and the comfortable middle class (200 million) put together. If elections are about arithmetic, it is this demographic which will decide who governs India next.

It has taken a while for politics and indeed the intelligentsia to recognise that there aren't two Indias: the old dichotomy between the prosperous India of the big cities and deprived Bharat of the villages. There are, in fact, three Indias, the largest of which lives neither in big cities nor in decrepit villages, but in rural–urban continuums across the length and breadth of India. It is this segment that is highly aspirational and impatient for a better quality of life. And every major political formation has trouble capturing its imagination.

The Congress never realised that it was this demographic, which grew exponentially during UPA-I's high growth rate tenure, which delivered it a second term—the Congress did very well outside the deep recesses of rural India. That is why, despite Rahul Gandhi's articulation of the seventy crore, the party has nothing to offer them. The Congress is still very much focused on the bottom 300 million—that is the segment which is most likely to be appreciative of the rights-based/doles-based policy approach that the grand old party over-emphasises.

Arvind Kejriwal had the ears of this demographic when he stormed into politics. His promise to eradicate corruption appealed most to this neo-middle class—after all the rich paid bribes, and the poor never had any access to the system at all. Arguably, Kejriwal's style of populism in the form of the promise of cheap power and free water also appealed to this class, more than the Congress's bare subsistence NREGA or Right to Food. Where Kejriwal lost out mainly was in his unseemly hurry. He certainly lost the upper middle classes, but by throwing away his opportunity in Delhi, he left his neo-middle class base disappointed and disillusioned. Additionally, there were a slew of corruption charges against his party colleagues, and absurd drama unfolding at his doorstep almost every day. For a person who had promised deliverance to the common man, he swiftly turned into a chief minister who shall be best remembered for his disruptionist style.

Perhaps unsurprisingly, Narendra Modi has done the most to capture the imagination of this segment. He has promised a better, more prosperous life to this seventy crore. A future of skills, jobs and material well being. If Modi has a problem, it lies in the (hitherto limited) ability of his political rivals to paint him as someone whose philosophy of governance favours the twenty crore middle class and not the seventy crore neo-middle class. But the fact that Modi (who rose in life from abject poverty) is seen as more representative of this group than a Rahul Gandhi or Arvind Kejriwal helps neutralise some of the criticism of him being pro-rich.

That isn't to argue that Modi has a complete stranglehold on this demographic. There are political parties and leaders in parts of India who can compete (and beat) Modi for this neo-middle class vote. It is when a leader or party has been able to convey a message of change and prosperity that he or she has captured this group's vote. In varying degrees, the late J. Jayalalithaa, Naveen Patnaik, and Mamata Banerjee won this demographic in their states. In Uttar Pradesh, the youthful Akhilesh Yadav had captured the imagination of the 'not poor, not rich' in 2012, but in his spectacular failure to provide governance, ceded much ground to Modi which resulted in BJP's victory and the anointment of Chief Minister Yogi Adityanath.

All those who end up on the losing side in 2019 will certainly introspect and recalibrate their strategies for the future. The voters of the 'third' India ought to be at the core of a rethink.

(This article was first published in *Firstpost.com*)

MAKING 'MAKE IN INDIA' WORK

This article was first published in December 2014, some months after Prime Minister Modi announced an ambitious Make in India programme to boost manufacturing in India. Unlike many other emerging economies, especially in East Asia, India has failed to develop a strong manufacturing base, particularly in job-generating, low-technology industries like apparel and footwear. This article presents the arguments for the necessary ingredients for success. Four years down, much of the work remains to be done.

Prime Minister Narendra Modi's flagship 'Make in India' campaign is an effort to boost India's manufacturing sector to China-like levels.

The conventional wisdom is that the only way to find jobs for a young and growing population, and to move workers off the farm and into cities, is to expand India's export-focused industries. That's the same route Japan, China and the so-called Asian Tigers all pursued successfully. Yet, does the world really need another export powerhouse? With demand in developed nations slowing, there simply may not be enough customers for Indian-made goods, no matter how cheap. The alternative—stimulating domestic demand artificially, by raising tariffs on imports—has been tried and failed spectacularly under previous socialist governments.

Even if one agrees with the goal of boosting manufacturing, the government has yet to offer any convincing strategies for achieving it. Modi placed great emphasis on raising India's ranking in the World Bank's Ease of Doing Business survey. That required taking an axe to India's tangle of red tape: simplifying processes for opening a business and for registering property; improving the enforcement of contracts and collection of taxes; making it easier to acquire permits.

Yet while businesses would happily embrace such changes, they're unlikely to unleash a manufacturing revolution. Like China, India has already tried to implement several of these reforms in Special Economic Zones (SEZ) that advertise lower taxes and looser land and labour regulations. These efforts have yet to amount to much, at least partly due to weak demand in advanced countries.

The real problem is that markets for four critical inputs for manufacturing, or indeed any business—land, labour, power and capital—are badly distorted. Until the government resolves those distortions, 'Make in India' will remain nothing but a slogan.

Consider land. A new land acquisition law, passed in the dying months of the previous government in 2013, makes buying farmland on which to build factories tremendously complicated and expensive; by law, companies have to pay four times the market price in rural areas. There's simply no free market for land in India.

On labour, India should have a cost advantage over China, whose labour-intensive goods now flood the Indian market. Chinese wages have risen rapidly over three decades of double-digit growth. India's haven't, and almost half the population is still engaged in unproductive agriculture. Yet tough labour laws mean that the opportunity costs of hiring workers remain cripplingly high. While the government has started a debate on reforming those laws, few changes are evident yet.

Unreliable and expensive power supplies hamper all of India's businesses. Indian governments have long subsidised agriculture and regular consumers by charging higher rates to industry. China and other emerging nations have followed the opposite strategy. India need not reverse course completely, but it needs at least to even out prices for everyone while boosting overall supply.

Compared to the rest of the world, Indian interest rates tend to be too high even when monetary policy is more accommodative. There's also plenty more room for India to open up its financial system, even if it remains wary of the kind of cowboy capitalism that led to the 2008 crash.

The government can help manufacturers by following through on pledges to invest in roads, ports and connectivity. But only when India's markets for land, labour, power and capital work efficiently, will the foundations for a true cost-competitive manufacturing revolution exist. Indian companies shouldn't need any special protections to compete with cheap Chinese goods at home. And when the advanced economies finally recover, there will be other markets to conquer.

(This article was first published in *Bloomberg View*.)

NEEDED, BANKING REFORMS

This article was written in 2014 after Prime Minister Modi announced the Jan Dhan Yojana to extend access of the banking system to every Indian. Universal financial inclusion must be a prerequisite for a functioning market economy. Four years on, the Jan Dhan Yojana has achieved universal coverage for all households. There has been considerable movement forward on Direct Benefit Transfers which will put money directly into the bank accounts of those Indians who need it most. The second part of the financial reform agenda, relating to the mainstream banking sector, is still in progress. The state of public sector banks is dire because of non-performing assets. Even private sector banks are not immune to this problem. However, the new bankruptcy law and the decision to recapitalise public sector banks has begun to ease the stress on the banking system. True financial inclusion requires healthy banks to lend at reasonable rates to a maximum number of citizens and businesses. In the long run, this requires much greater competition and privatisation of at least a part of the government-owned banking system.

Universal access to the banking system is a pre-requisite for a modern economy. And yet, forty-seven years after banks were nationalised apparently to meet this objective, only 400 million Indians have access to a bank account. In fact, twice that number owns a mobile phone. In that context, it is hard to find fault with Prime Minister Narendra Modi's Jan Dhan Yojana, even if it smacks of populism. If indeed the offers of an overdraft facility of 5,000 rupees, life insurance worth 30,000 rupees, and accident insurance worth one lakh encourage people to open a bank account, it would be money well spent.

A logical next step would be for the government to move to direct cash transfers in all its varied subsidy/largesse schemes.

The one major hindrance to cash transfers, which are infinitely more efficient in reaching the targeted beneficiaries than existing systems which rely on corrupt middlemen, was that the poor did not have bank accounts. An aggressively implemented Jan Dhan Yojana could solve that problem and a lot of others for Finance Minister Arun Jaitley. He will then have the opportunity to implement a radical overhaul of the government's expensive and leaky benefits system. It would be the best medicine for the fiscal deficit and it would also be popular as the most deserving people will receive their dues without hassle or hustle. Needless to say, it will also please banks, which would otherwise complain about the costs of servicing mostly inactive accounts.

It is important to recognise that access to a bank account isn't the end of any financial inclusion drive. Actually, it only ought to be the beginning.

Meaningful financial inclusion must warrant access to credit at reasonable rates. For that, the Indian financial system needs to be made competitive. That would require ending the dominance of public sector banks, which do a brilliant job of giving bad loans to the well-connected and a terrible job of giving loans to the proverbial aam aadmi.

Privatisation may be a bridge too far, but the government should encourage the entry of many more private sector banks, whether domestic or foreign. At least some of these new entrants will tap the massive market at the bottom of the pyramid. In 2014, the RBI granted a banking licence to Bandhan, which was extensively involved in microfinance. That could be a role model to follow when thinking about genuine financial inclusion.

Of course, any reform of the banking system will require Prime Minister Modi to bite the bullet. The aftermath of the global financial crisis has created a cosy consensus that Indian banking is in fine fettle and radical reform would only destabilise it. Nothing could be further from the truth. Just look at the nonperforming assets of the major banks which have grown steadily in the last five years. If Modi can match the populism of the Jan Dhan Yojana with some serious reform of mainstream banking, he will have achieved what no government in Independent India has—real and universal financial inclusion.

(This article was first published in *The Sunday Guardian.*)

MODI'S LITTLE BANG REFORMS

This article was first published in October 2014 shortly after the BJP won important elections in the states of Maharashtra and Haryana where it had never previously installed chief ministers. It was also a period in which the commentariat was concerned about the lack of major structural reforms in the first six months of the new government. This piece makes the argument that in India's complex political economy, which is also in a perpetual cycle of elections, big bang reforms are never likely to materialise. Small steps towards reforms are good enough, provided the government does not make major mistakes. Four years on, there is enough evidence to suggest that the Modi government has proceeded in the right reformist direction without many mistakes. The revival of growth in an environment of stable inflation and in a cleaner system is proof that continuous reform in the right direction is good for growth.

For Indian Prime Minister Narendra Modi, Diwali came early in 2014 when his Bharatiya Janata Party won crucial elections in the states of Maharashtra and Haryana. He's celebrated with a bang—a little one.

On 18 October, a day before election results were announced, Modi's government deregulated retail diesel prices. On 20 October, the administration issued an ordinance intended to sort out the mess in India's coal industry, which had been thrown into turmoil by the Supreme Court's decisions. Many supporters expected bigger things from Modi: perhaps a lifting of all fuel and fertiliser subsidies, or the privatisation of state-owned Coal India. Modi's more modest reforms, however, may be a smarter way for India to move forward.

Expectations that the forceful Modi would suddenly rip up decades of bad policy after taking power were always overblown. The prime minister seems intent instead on working through gradual, calibrated changes to India's decaying policy framework. Take the ordinance on coal. A Supreme Court ruling invalidating the allocation of over 200 coal blocks handed out since 1993 left dozens of private companies in doubt about their power supplies. The government decided to reassign those blocks using a transparent, online auction rather than a murky and easily corrupted bidding process.

The power, steel and cement companies that depend on these coal supplies now have a degree of clarity. Coal-rich states will benefit, as their governments will get the revenue from the auctions rather than New Delhi.

The ordinance falls far short of denationalising the coal sector, which is ultimately the only way to solve India's perennial power shortages. But any such move would inevitably have failed, given that Modi's party still lacks a majority in the upper house of parliament. Worse, a futile attempt would probably have derailed even smaller-bore reforms of the sector. The new ordinance contains an enabling clause that recognises the need to open up coal mining to private competition.

The prime minister doesn't need upper-house approval to lift fuel, food and fertiliser subsidies, which together account for a third of India's huge fiscal deficit. The regulation of diesel prices was a particular scandal, benefitting mostly rich SUV drivers and truck transportation companies. Ending it—especially while global oil prices are depressed—was a no-brainer.

To go further, however, would also have provoked crippling resistance. Raising the prices of cooking gas and kerosene, both overwhelmingly used by India's hundreds of millions of poor, without setting up a buffer of some sort would have been irresponsible and rightly opposed. Modi says he plans to rationalise those subsidies by replacing them with cash transfers to the poorest citizens; the same would apply to food and fertiliser subsidies. First making sure that the transfer system is workable and uncorrupted makes good political as well as policy sense.

This style of incremental reform may be too slow to propel India back to double-digit growth, as some fear. But the overhang of bad policies in India is too acute to be solved in a matter of months. Unlike his predecessors, Modi at least isn't creating any bad new policies. In India, that counts as progress.

(This article was first published in *Bloomberg View.*)

WHY DOESN'T INDIA HAVE ITS OWN SILICON VALLEY?

The world's cutting edge and most exciting companies have been born in the capitalism of America's Silicon Valley. However, India's impressive technology companies which grew in the free market environment of Bengaluru haven't quite achieved global domination. This article first published in September 2015 argues that India is still too over regulated for genuine world beaters to emerge. India's IT companies grew in a vacuum because the government did not regulate IT services in the 1980s while it was stifling hardware. Modi's government has done much to foster an innovation ecosystem. The Atal Innovation Mission is putting Tinkering labs in schools all over the country so that future generations grow up with a mind-set of innovation. The Startup India programme is encouraging first generation entrepreneurs. But work remains to be done on further easing the environment of doing business as well as upgrading the skill and research ecosystems.

Two of the planet's most powerful technology companies have CEOs of Indian origin: Microsoft's Satya Nadella and Google's Sundar Pichai. Indeed, one study found that fifteen per cent of all Silicon Valley start-ups in 2012 were led by

Indians, even though they comprised only six per cent of the area's population.

The question Modi should ask himself is this: why hasn't India been able to replicate, even in some small measure, Silicon Valley's top-end technology ecosystem? Why haven't Indians been able to create a Google or Facebook in Bengaluru?

The question may sound counter-intuitive. If there's one thing India is known for abroad, besides poverty, it's the country's prowess in Information Technology. How often have you heard the assertion that if China is the factory of the world, India is its back office? Modi has repeated the boast; so has China's President Xi Jinping.

In that claim, though, lies a partial explanation for why India's technology scene remains underdeveloped. Beginning in the 1980s, Indian tech companies focused on providing relatively low value-added IT services to overseas clients, rather than developing high value-added products. The choice made sense. Companies faced a tough climate for doing business in then-socialist India and a small domestic market. Red tape strangled the hardware sector, as so many others in India; archaic labour laws and a lack of power discouraged new factories. Given India's nationalised banking system, financing for risky start-ups was slim-to-non-existent.

By contrast, the tech services sector was virtually unregulated. While not as well-trained and innovative as in the US, India's pool of engineers was large, low-cost and English-speaking. Companies such as Infosys and Wipro could set up private generators to power their Bengaluru campuses and could grow far away from the watchful eyes of Delhi bureaucrats.

India's IT giants may be victims of their own success. At least until the global economic crisis hit in 2008, Infosys, Tata

Consultancy Services, HCL and Wipro were hugely profitable and globally respected. They never had to develop the risk appetite to branch out into higher-end services, let alone product development.

At the same time, the hype over the Bengaluru boom obscured the fact that India hadn't really created a true start-up ecosystem. Silicon Valley, for instance, benefits greatly from the presence of several top-notch universities; academic research is translated quickly into the real world, while feedback travels in the other direction. Yet despite setting up fourteen new Indian Institutes of Technology (IITs) since the 1990s, successive Indian governments haven't seen fit to locate one in Bengaluru itself. (Modi's proposed putting one in Dharwad, a town more than 400 kilometres away.) Meanwhile, India spends only 0.8 per cent of its GDP on research and development, compared to 2.8 per cent in the US, and 1.8 per cent in China, both of which have much higher GDPs than India. Until relatively recently, Indian start-ups attracted limited venture capital and private equity funding compared to their Chinese counterparts. Intellectual property protections were weak.

After the financial crisis dried up demand, companies such as Infosys and HCL responded by seeking to move up the value chain. Infosys, which appointed Vishal Sikka, a high-ranking executive at Germany's SAP as CEO in 2014, is now pursuing advances in automation, Artificial Intelligence and design.

Still, any true tech pioneer is more likely to emerge from outside the circle of Bengaluru's giants. In the last few years, a clutch of internet-based start-ups has begun to take advantage of a sector that is today as lightly regulated as IT services were three decades ago. Their young entrepreneurs have shown a greater appetite for risk than their predecessors. Perhaps more importantly, they've benefited from the emergence of a new set of VC and private equity investors willing to stake capital and nurture businesses over the long-term. New e-commerce players such as Flipkart and Snapdeal have attracted investments valuing them at 15.5 billion US dollars, and 4.8 billion dollars in 2015, respectively. Zomato, a restaurant search-and-discovery service founded in 2008, received over 200 million dollars in funding and now has a presence in over twenty countries.

Flipkart and Snapdeal are still small companies by the standards of world leader Amazon and China's Alibaba, of course. And for now, they're focused on expanding their Indian footprint rather than expanding globally. But the fact that they enjoy a huge domestic market (today's India is much richer than India in 1985) means that they've got a good shot at developing products and technology that could have much wider appeal.

If Modi really wants India to produce an Apple or Amazon, though, he needs to focus on improving the environment for innovation at home—cutting regulations, investing in research and education, and boosting growth in order to expand the domestic market. Indians abroad are obviously talented and nimble enough to innovate. The question is whether India is, too.

(This article was first published in *Bloomberg View.*)

WHERE THINGS ARE WORKING IN INDIA

It is commonplace to think that the only government India has is the one in New Delhi. The fact is that in India's federal system, the Union Government is complemented by twenty-nine state governments. This article published in September 2015 is a reminder of the important Constitutionally-mandated role played by state governments in the process of market reforms. While this article focusses on the ease of doing business reforms, states have to take a lead in implementing other reforms so essential for the flourishing of a market economy, including running a good schools system, efficient healthcare and sound law and order. Competition between states and replication of best practices can have a force multiplier effect on reforms in India even if the Union Government moves at a slower pace.

It's only natural for investors to think of India as a whole: the sheer size and unity of its market is a large part of the country's appeal. Yet, what matters most to companies are conditions in the individual states where they run their businesses. And here, when one looks at the policies being promoted by India's twenty-nine state governments, one can discern more reason for optimism—and a better sense of what still needs to improve.

In October 2017, for the first time, a study conducted by the World Bank in cooperation with KPMG and the government's Make in India initiative ranked Indian states in terms of the ease of doing business—improving which is one of Prime Minister Narendra Modi's highest priorities. Each state was asked to report how many of the ninety-eight reforms suggested by Modi's government they had adopted, in eight broad categories: setting up a business; allotment of land and obtaining a construction permit; complying with environmental procedures; complying with labour regulations; obtaining infrastructure-related utilities; registering and complying with tax procedures; carrying out inspections; enforcing contracts.

The best news is that setting goals seems to have had an effect. The study notes that most of the reforms it registered were implemented in just the first half of the year. That suggests, contrary to perception, that there's new momentum behind reform, at least in the realm of processes.

Not surprisingly, the survey also revealed striking differences between states. Gujarat, Modi's home state and a long time pace-setter in reforms, came out on top with a seventy-one per cent compliance rate. Indeed, BJP or its allies, who presumably have more of an incentive to fulfil the prime minister's priorities, rule seven out of the top eight states.

Interestingly though, there's little correlation between a state's per capita income and its reformist credentials. Rich states like Punjab, Haryana and even Delhi appear in the middle of the rankings, while relatively poor states such as Madhya Pradesh, Chhattisgarh and Odisha score much better. If their laggard status is pushing them to reform faster, that's good news for India.

The rankings also give a clear indication of what works. Areas where state governments have been able to shift procedures online—most notably, in tax collection—have improved the most. By switching to transparent, web-based systems, the best-performing states have streamlined procedures for winning construction permits, approving building plans and allotting land.

Conversely, those areas where bureaucrats still wield great influence—and which have the greatest potential for bribery and cronyism—are the slowest to change. India's notorious inspectors continue to harass companies to check for violations of regulations covering everything from paying wages to chopping down trees. Decisive reform in this sphere would require taking on powerful vested interests, something India's political parties across the board seem unwilling to risk.

Clearly, there remains much work to be done: as many as sixteen states had compliance rates of below twenty-five per cent. Some of these are constrained by difficult geographies which would make attracting investment difficult. Seven of those sixteen states are in India's somewhat isolated and land-locked Northeast; three are mountainous Himalayan states.

Indeed, one hope is that rankings such as this one will spur competition among states. In one of the most heartening developments in recent years, voters have much more consistently rewarded state governments that have delivered jobs and development and voted out those that have not. Eventually, as some states race ahead and attract projects and investment, the laggards will feel pressure to follow suit.

Obviously, if India's states grow quickly, so will the country. Yet none of this absolves Modi's government of its responsibility. Exporters such as Foxconn may only need to find one or two efficient states in order to set up factories in India. But companies catering to the domestic market will struggle unless broader reforms—like the recent Goods and Services Tax that knits the country together into a true single market—are implemented. Modi's task remains as daunting as ever.

(This article was first published in *Bloomberg View.*)

HOW TO END INDIA'S TAX TERRORISM

The thriving of a market economy depends centrally on robust private investment. Perhaps there is nothing which worries entrepreneurs and investors more about India than its tax system. This article published in April 2015 warned the Modi government of the pitfalls of an adversarial tax system. Since then, the government has eased corporate tax rates but businesses continue to suffer from a complex tax administration system. Demonetisation and GST, important reform measures, have empowered the tax departments without any radical reform of the administration system. This has to be a priority of Modi's government going forward if double-digit growth is to be achieved. Investors need to be assured that the tax system will be predictable and fair.

Under Prime Minister Narendra Modi, the government has gone to great lengths to distinguish itself from the supposedly anti-business policies of its predecessor. Finance Minister Arun Jaitley assured foreign companies and investors that India would no longer engage in 'tax terrorism'—suddenly levying huge retrospective tax bills on corporations such as Vodafone, which was charged with more than two billion US dollars in back taxes in 2012.

But the government is in danger of undoing any goodwill

it might have earned. Rather than moving to repeal the 2012 law that allowed for the retrospective charges on Vodafone, Jaitley merely said that the government would no longer apply it. And in 2015, Cairn India, an oil exploration company owned by the UK-based Vedanta group, was slapped with a tax notice worth 3.6 billion US dollars for a transaction that occurred in 2006–07 (well before Vedanta bought the company). Indian officials claim Cairn did not pay capital gains tax for a set of transactions that involved the transfer of shares from its UK parent to its Indian subsidiary.

A second case is even more egregious. Tax authorities issued notices to collect 6.4 billion US dollars in taxes from a group of a hundred Foreign Institutional Investors (FIIs) for the year 2012–13. The investors were being penalised under something called the Minimum Alternative Tax, a twenty per cent levy that's meant to apply to companies who would otherwise pay zero corporate tax because of various exemptions and deductions.

So far, the levy had never been applied to foreign investors, only to entities that had business income in India. (FIIs pay a Securities Transaction Tax and a fifteen per cent capital gains tax on securities held for less than a year.) Jaitley specifically said that the tax would not apply to FIIs. India's tax officials insist that Jaitley's change applies only prospectively; their demand is retrospective. Worse, notices may be issued to several other FIIs on the same grounds.

Arun Jaitley has tried to argue that foreigners cannot expect India to be a tax haven: legitimate taxes must be paid. But advising unhappy companies to take their cases to court, as Jaitley has done, is no solution. The molasses-slow judicial system only prolongs uncertainty.

The basic problem is the morass of Indian tax laws, a legacy of the socialist era. The system is adversarial and tilted towards enforcement rather than compliance. Ridiculously high rates of direct taxes—topping ninety per cent in the 1970s—were gradually reduced through the 1980s and 1990s. But even then, corporate tax rates between thirty and forty per cent stood well above those in competitor nations. To incentivise the private sector, policy makers have tried to bypass the system with a maze of deductions and exemptions. While these may have boosted some sectors, they've also created ambiguity and opportunities for rent-seeking.

Additionally, they have also led to a lopsided scenario where large, profitable firms pay lower taxes than smaller, less profitable ones. The government's 2015 budget documents revealed that the effective tax rate for firms whose profits are above a hundred million US dollars is 20.68 per cent, while the same rate for firms with a profit of 1,70,000 dollars is 26.89 per cent (both are lower than the actual corporate tax rate of thirty per cent). The fact that the country needs a Minimum Alternate Tax at all is a symbol of all that's wrong with the system: the levy wouldn't exist if loopholes didn't allow some corporations to avoid tax altogether.

Modi's government is caught in its own trap. It wants to stick to the letter of the law even as it acknowledges that those laws are counterproductive. It's possible the prospect of extra revenue is too tempting to resist for a government looking to ramp up spending; Jaitley has said that he could use the 6.4 billion dollars from foreign investors to solve India's irrigation problems. Or possibly, the government may be concerned about being labelled pro-business and is going out of its way to prove that it's not.

Whatever the reason, the outcome threatens to torpedo

investor confidence. What's needed is a dramatic overhaul of the tax code. Instead of applying bad laws indiscriminately, Jaitley and his taxmen should invest their energies in simplifying the system. That's where he should concentrate his efforts, not in holding up companies and investors for what looks disturbingly like ransom.

(This article was first published in *Bloomberg View.*)

INDIA'S MISSING INVESTORS

A vibrant stock market has been one of the marked success of post-liberalisation India. And yet, too few Indians invest in stocks. This article published in April 2015 noted the huge boom in the stock market in the year after Prime Minister Modi assumed office. However, retail investor participation in the prosperity generated by this boom was small. The need to attract more individuals to equities is fundamental. Indians tend to invest in non-productive assets like gold and real estate rather than investing in businesses which will generate returns for the economy as a whole. For a high growth economy, savings need to be channelled to productive outlets. For this the government needs to educate its citizens and build trust through first rate regulation of stock markets.

If Prime Minister Narendra Modi delivered one thing in his first ten months in office, it's been electricity to India's stock markets. India's benchmark, Bombay Stock Exchange (BSE) Sensex recorded a thirty-one per cent jump in 2014. Only the insane run-up in Shanghai's bourse—up ninety per cent then—overshadowed the Indian rally.

Unfortunately, very few actual Indians stand to benefit from the boom. The proportion of retail investors in India's equities markets is strikingly low. Less than 1.5 per cent of the population invests in securities, compared with almost ten per cent in China and eighteen per cent in the US. Just two per cent of India's household savings are exposed to equity; in the US, the long-term average is forty-five per cent.

This is ultimately bad news for India's economy. The country desperately needs to channel more household savings into equities—which are a vital source of corporate finance—and away from unproductive investments in gold and real estate. India also needs more local funds if it's to sustain the strength in its equities market while avoiding macroeconomic imbalances. At the moment, around seventy per cent of the market is dominated by Foreign Institutional Investors.

Consider this statistic. Between September 2008 and October 2014, those foreign investors made net purchases of forty-five billion US dollars. In the same period, domestic institutional investors (mostly funded by retail investors) made net sales of sixteen billion dollars. This imbalance creates serious side effects. The billions of dollars flowing in produce upward pressure on the rupee and a decline in India's competitiveness. When they flow out, usually at short notice, markets collapse and the exchange rate grows volatile. That scenario is almost certain to play out when the US Fed tightens monetary policy.

At one level, the reluctance of retail investors doesn't make sense. Despite the normal ups and downs, India's markets have done well over the last decade. The Sensex gave a return of seventeen per cent compounded annually between August 2004 and August 2014. That's twice as much as Indians earn from their most preferred mode of financial savings: bank deposits. Yet the proportion of retail turnover to total turnover actually declined from over eighty per cent in 2003 to under thirty-five per cent in 2013.

What accounts for the disillusionment? For one thing, retail investors may not have earned the average rate of return. Like mom-and-pop investors in other countries, most notably China, India's punters don't always make the best buy-and-sell decisions. They usually sell high-performing stock earlier than they should and hold onto badly-performing ones too long. They also tend to enter stock markets near their peaks and quickly lose confidence when they fall. Also, the one market which usually attracts retail investors in larger numbers—the market for initial public offerings—has performed poorly in India over the last decade. An analysis of 394 IPOs between 2003 and 2014 found that only 164 companies were trading over their offer price. Thus, sixty per cent of investors lost money over a decade.

There's also a lingering perception that India's stock markets are manipulated by a few big players; markets have been marred by several high-profile scams in the last two decades. While India's stock market regulator has done a reasonable job of reining in malpractices, confidence still lags. Also, India's dominant family-run companies, as well as listed public sector companies, need to offer more of their stock to the public to add depth to what's traded and to make manipulation harder. Many have struggled to comply with the requirement that at least a quarter of shares be publicly held.

The development of a robust Indian equity market after 1991 represents one of the great achievements of India's liberalisation policies. To reap the full gains, though, the government now needs to do a better job of educating and enticing its own citizens into taking part.

(This article was first published in *Bloomberg View.*)

TO SPEND IN INDIA, FIRST CUT TAXES

This article was published in February 2015 just before Modi's government presented its second Union Budget. The argument made in this article is as valid today as it was then. Too few Indians pay tax because of a long history of high tax rates. This means that the government has less revenue to spend on important sectors like education, health and sanitation. However, the way to increase the tax base is not to raise rates but to lower them so that compliance increases. Unfortunately, a defensive tax bureaucracy has not permitted serious tax cuts. The multi-slab GST was a missed opportunity for lowering the incidence of indirect taxation. The argument for lower tax rates must continue to be made by linking it to an improved tax base and a greater, not lesser, ability of the government to spend.

No single budget can solve or even tackle the full range of problems that afflict India's sputtering economy. The most powerful reform Modi could introduce might also be one of the most popular: cutting taxes. This might sound counter-intuitive, given India's continuing fiscal pressures. But handled correctly, lowering overall tax rates should lead to a boost in revenue.

The government is facing renewed populist pressures. The BJP's crushing defeat in Delhi's state elections—to a Left-leaning party that offered a variety of freebies to voters—ended its string of impressive state-level performances since Modi's inauguration. The temptation for the government is obviously to minimise pain in the budget, perhaps even to expand wasteful subsidy programmes.

Instead the government should slash income taxes. Currently, barely three per cent of India's 1.25 billion people pay income tax. That figure is absurdly low even considering the hundreds of millions of poor who are exempt. Even the most pessimistic estimates suggest they account for no more than thirty per cent of the population.

In the late 1970s, India's top tax rate exceeded ninety per cent, and most wealthy Indians conducted as much of their business as possible off the books in order to evade the tax man. Unsurprisingly, by 1991 the country's direct tax-to-GDP ratio (which includes both corporate and income taxes) stood at a paltry 1.9 per cent. With the onset of economic liberalisation, tax rates were lowered, which helped encourage more middle-class Indians to pay up. The direct tax-to-GDP ratio has improved to 5.6 per cent. Combined with a reduction of loopholes and more transparent collection efforts, lower taxes should buoy revenues over the medium term.

The last radical cut in corporate and income taxes took place eighteen years ago, when the latter were divided into three 'slabs': ten per cent, twenty per cent, and thirty per cent. Since then, instead of reducing rates, the government has increased the number of people exempt from paying tax to those earning less than 3,00,000 rupees (roughly 5,000 US dollars) per year. Surcharges have been added to the top rate in an attempt to boost revenues. The government should also impose a moratorium on increasing the exemption limit, so that more Indians are drawn into the tax net.

This is not, on the other hand, an opportune moment to reduce corporate taxes, which are thirty-four per cent for most companies. While that rate is comparable to France and Japan and lower than the US, it is much higher than some emerging economies like China, Malaysia and Indonesia (twenty-five per cent) or Russia (twenty per cent). For India to be competitive, the rate needs to come down. However, Modi already has a reputation for favouring India's big industrialists, who were major contributors to his campaign. Now, he can't afford to look like he's coddling the rich.

Leaving corporate rates where they are should also minimise any losses to the exchequer. In the meantime, the government could move to simplify the needlessly complex corporate tax structure. Eliminating surcharges would bring the rate down to thirty per cent. The government could also begin to lift sector-specific exemptions which have encouraged rent-seeking and tax evasion. This would set the stage for a reduction in the corporate tax rate to twenty-five per cent, or even twenty per cent, over the next four years.

A more transparent direct tax system with moderate rates and no exemptions would greatly boost India's competitiveness, as well as GDP. It would be unrealistic to accomplish all of this in one sweep, of course. But Modi would be wise to get started on the task.

(This article was first published in *Bloomberg View*.)

MODI NEEDS A FARM FIX

This article was first published in April 2015 and urged the government of Prime Minister Modi to address the stress in India's agriculture. At least one of the measures recommended in this article was implemented by the government, but its success on the ground is mixed. The fact is that even in 2018, agriculture continues to be a challenge for policymakers. Perhaps one reason for this is insufficient trust in market forces. Agriculture needs less government intervention, particularly in the setting of prices and quantities. Government's focus needs to be on providing income support (which doesn't distort prices) and building rural infrastructure, particularly irrigation, in a country in which a lot of agriculture is still dependent on the monsoon. What needs to end is perverse intervention like export bans or mandi monopolies which cost the farmer. To be fair, the government has a dilemma between assuring higher incomes to farmers and keeping food prices low for consumers. But that conflict isn't solved by dabbling in price-fixing but by finding other ways to boost farmer income, especially from non-crop sources like animal husbandry, through the sharing economy in farming equipment and the facilitation of rural industries. The government's stated commitment to double farmers' income by 2022 has a large dose of market reform as part of the agenda.

Optimists are in the ascendant in India, where Prime Minister Narendra Modi's reform efforts spurred predictions of 7.5

per cent growth in 2015—higher even than China. By contrast, the country's most eminent agricultural economist warned that growth in the farming sector was likely to flat-line. That may not cripple the larger economy, since agriculture now accounts for only fifteen per cent of India's GDP. But it's catastrophic for the one in two Indians who depend on farming for a living.

Clearly, Modi's initiatives have had no direct impact on India's long-suffering farmers. One could argue that past efforts to improve their lot have turned out to be little more than boondoggles, where most of the gains end up in the pockets of unscrupulous middlemen. And it's true that the government's main focus should be to encourage a manufacturing industry that can draw the huge surplus of unproductive workers off the land and into towns and cities.

Still, Modi can hardly afford to look on idly as half the population suffers. Unseasonal rains damage crops heavily. There have been several reports of farmer suicides. In the twenty-first century, Indian peasants remain far too vulnerable to the whims of the weather gods: too much rain is as disastrous as too little, or as a badly distributed monsoon.

One simple way to cushion the blow better would be for the government to introduce crop insurance. In its 2015 budget, the government instituted subsidised accident and life insurance schemes for the poor. Modi ought to launch a similar programme for farmers, insuring they won't be wiped out if bad weather destroys their crops.

Still, insurance is only a short-term palliative. More radical reform is necessary, not least because agriculture has an outsized impact on macroeconomic stability. Double-digit inflation between 2010 and 2014 was caused largely by a massive run up in agricultural prices. The threat is pernicious: the central bank's usual tool for tackling inflation—adjusting interest rates—is a blunt instrument for dealing with what are in effect structural supply constraints in the farm sector.

Modi hasn't been as creative and bold about agriculture as he has been about manufacturing. In fact, his election pledge to raise the government-set 'minimum support price' for rice and wheat—promising farmers a profit of fifty per cent over cost—was an outright terrible idea. The idea of guaranteeing farmers an unreasonably high floor cost for growing specific crops distorts the entire sector. It incentivises farmers to grow cereals regardless of soil and weather patterns. That in turn reduces production of fruits and vegetables, scarcity of which drives India's food inflation.

Given the voting power of farmers, State-determined procurement prices are a one-way street: they always go up. That, too, feeds into inflationary expectations. And given their relative poverty, inflation pinches most farmers and farm workers even more than it does the urban middle class. Rather than guaranteeing prices, the government should guarantee a minimum level of income, transferred directly through cash subsidies. That would free up farmers to grow riskier but potentially more lucrative crops.

The government also needs to rethink the system of State-run wholesale markets, where farmers are required to sell their produce at auction. Originally set up to prevent poorly educated peasants from being exploited by middlemen, these markets have given rise to local monopolies; farmers have little bargaining power against traders. Modi could begin by pressing the states run by his Bharatiya Janata Party to introduce private markets, giving farmers a choice about where to sell.

Vested interests will resist these changes, not to mention more far-reaching reforms such as allowing direct foreign investment in retail, which would revolutionise the supply chain from farmers to stores. Both to prevent inflation and needless suffering, though, Modi should make them a priority.

(This article was first published in *Bloomberg View.*)

INDIA'S FACTORY FUTURE

It is easy to be pessimistic about the future of manufacturing in India, given the limited success that has been achieved so far. However, as this article published in September 2014 points out, there is a ready model in India of a manufacturing powerhouse: Gujarat. While it is not easy to replicate Gujarat's geography or long history of entrepreneurship in every part of India, it is feasible to create an enabling environment for enterprise that the state has done. It is a task that must be carried out by the state governments in particular since Gujarat has achieved manufacturing success under a Union Government policy framework that is the same for all of India.

China's President Xi Jinping played to stereotype in 2014 when he described his country as the world's factory and India as the world's back office in an op-ed article heralding his arrival in the latter. How ironic then that Xi's first port of call wasn't Bengaluru, the heart of India's outsourcing industry. It was instead Ahmedabad—the largest city in Gujarat state, which can justifiably lay claim to being India's factory.

Consider the numbers. In China, industry contributes forty-four per cent to Gross Domestic Product, compared with only twenty-six per cent in India. By contrast, services add fifty-seven per cent to GDP in India, versus only forty-six per cent in China.

(The difference is made up by agriculture.) In that sense, Xi's description is valid.

In Gujarat, however, industry contributes forty-one per cent of the state's GDP, while agriculture and services add thirteen per cent and forty-six per cent, respectively. This corner of western India is already a manufacturing powerhouse—and a model that the rest of India should find easier to emulate than China's.

Gujarat officials signed a series of agreements to deepen cooperation with Guangdong, the coastal province that has been the engine of China's growth miracle. No doubt there's much that India can learn from the mainland's experience; at almost 900 billion US dollars, Guangdong's GDP is almost ten times that of Gujarat's ninety-six billion dollars.

Guangdong had unique advantages, though. China's then-leader, Deng Xiaoping chose the province to introduce economic reforms in 1978. The port city of Shenzhen, China's first Special Economic Zone, enjoyed geographical proximity to Hong Kong, a global economic hub. The province received major tax concessions, which it used to lure investors. China's authoritarian political system allowed employers to keep wages repressed, which became the foundation for a cheap manufacturing base.

None of this is realistic for India, where it would be impossible for the federal government to single out one state, like Gujarat, for special tax concessions. India's vibrant democracy wouldn't permit a repression of wages either, nor the kind of strict controls on migration from rural to urban areas that still exist in China to some extent.

And yet, Gujarat has succeeded. Sceptics argue that the state is atypical for India. It has a long coastline and a historically entrepreneurial population. Other states also have long coastlines, though. None except Maharashtra—which enjoys the luxury of hosting India's financial capital, Mumbai—and, to an extent, the southern state of Tamil Nadu have industrialised the way Gujarat has. Even Guangdong, a coastal province with a proud trading history, had little to show by way of industry before Deng's reforms. Policies matter.

Like Guangdong's, Gujarat's success is man-made. Even before India's current Prime Minister Narendra Modi took over as chief minister of the state in 2002, the local government had established a liberal policy regime for industry. Under Modi, the state continued to slash red tape and minimise corruption. Compared with the rest of India, companies can acquire land relatively easily; Gujarat regularly ranks at the top of Indian states in terms of economic freedom. The government has invested heavily in infrastructure, including good roads, 24x7 power, ports and airports. By contrast, Tamil Nadu suffers from acute power shortages. Maharashtra, outside of Mumbai, has awful infrastructure.

The so-called Gujarat Model may not be perfect. The state's human development indicators haven't entirely kept pace with economic growth. But it remains a promising test case, showing that the roadblocks to developing a manufacturing sector can largely be removed within the context of India's democratic system. Throttling bureaucracy can be scaled back; new power plants can be built. Indeed, Modi focused his entire election campaign around this promise—that he could replicate Gujarat's success on the national level.

It is up to him to prove Xi's stereotype wrong. To do so, the prime minister needs to liberalise the policy environment in New Delhi while devolving more authority and finances to states to improve their infrastructure. Modi needs to reform labour laws—which make it almost impossible to fire workers—and laws governing the acquisition of land; together those represent the two biggest obstacles to building a home-grown manufacturing sector in India. Investment from China, not to mention Japan and other nations, can help implement these policies, particularly when it comes to building infrastructure. But India shouldn't need inspiration, at least, from abroad.

(This article was first published in *Bloomberg View.*)

INDIA'S DRUG WAR IS GOOD NEWS

One of the outstanding successes of Indian capitalism has been the pharmaceuticals sector. This article was published in September 2014 at a time when there was a major disagreement within the ranks of India's pharmaceuticals industry on the issue of generic drugs. The fact is that the Indian pharma industry grew on the back of reverse engineering, previously discovered drugs, and selling them at a fraction of the price of global pharma MNCs. The split in 2014 showed that for the first time some India pharma companies were beginning to think beyond generics to move into the higher value added segments of the value chain. This showed that at least some Indian capitalists had the desire to become global leaders and not remain satisfied with where they were. Four years on, the trend can be seen in other industries too, especially IT which is also trying to move up the value chain as the returns from low-end services diminish.

The announcement that US pharmaceutical giant, Gilead would allow seven Indian companies to make a cheap, generic version of Sovaldi—its cure for the Hepatitis C virus and one of the world's best-selling drugs in 2014—was rightfully hailed as a victory for patients in the developing world. Instead of paying 84,000 US dollars for a twelve-week course of treatment as in the US, sufferers in India and ninety other nations will now be able to obtain a twenty-four-week course for less than 2,000 dollars.

So why were some of the loudest protests about the deal coming from the Indian pharmaceutical industry? The main industry lobby group, which represents the nineteen biggest Indian pharmaceutical firms, came out in opposition, despite the fact that three of its members signed the deal with Gilead. The Indian Pharmaceutical Alliance insists that the science behind Sovaldi is not new and hence not subject to patent—the same argument that allowed Indian drug makers to churn out some twenty-four billion dollars worth of other generics in 2013. The Alliance argued that dozens of India's 300 established pharmaceutical companies should be allowed to produce a version of Sovaldi, not just seven of them.

Ironically, Gilead's decision to choose Indian companies rather than those from other emerging economies, or even the US, was itself an acknowledgement of the competitiveness and skill of the local drug industry. It is the third largest in the world by volume and fourteenth by value (since generics are sold cheaply). Half of its revenues in 2013 were generated by exports to markets outside India. The country boasts the largest number of manufacturing facilities approved by the Food and Drug Administration outside the US.

Originally, Indian law only recognised process, not product patents. That paved the way for an explosion of copycat manufacturing between the 1970s and 1990s. World Trade Organisation rules later forced a change. But even now, Indian law has a loophole disallowing patents if the science behind the discovery is not new, or if a new drug represents merely a minor modification of an older drug.

The biggest Indian pharmaceutical companies would normally

have united behind this position. In recent years, however, the domestic market has grown brutally competitive. The top ten firms now command only thirty-seven per cent of the market, with no single player in double digits. The government imposes severe price controls on over 300 drugs, dampening profits. And many foreign markets remain closed to Indian-made knockoffs because of stronger patent protections.

The seven companies that signed up with Gilead, which include such familiar names as Cipla and Ranbaxy Laboratories, have clearly decided that they need to adopt a different strategy to maintain profitability. Not that long ago, Cipla dramatically challenged multinational drug companies, supplying a copycat cocktail of anti-HIV drugs to sub-Saharan African countries for 350 US dollars when their international market price was 15,000 dollars. Now, the prospect of bigger margins is simply too attractive to pass up.

A split in the Indian pharmaceutical industry isn't necessarily a bad thing for India or for the rest of the world. Critics have a fair point when they argue that 2,000 US dollars is still too expensive for patients in emerging economies, many of whom don't have access to insurance; the agreement also leaves out several key middle-income countries like China. But top Indian companies have to find ways to remain profitable. Some have tried to venture into original research, but the costs are high and the results unpredictable. Partnering with drug majors in the West—whether to produce cheaper versions of drugs or to conduct outsourced research and trials—is one obvious solution.

For the global pharmaceutical industry, the fact that some Indian companies are willing to look beyond rip-off generics opens up a host of possibilities. Drug discovery is expensive, and the prospects for future cures depend on keeping the profit incentive intact. At the same time, the pressure to sell at a discount in poorer countries is not going to go away. If the Western majors can outsource this task to cost-competitive Indian companies, while cutting back the threat of indiscriminate copycat versions, they might just be able to strike a balance between profit and social responsibility. Mostly everyone should win—or at least, more people than do under the current system.

(This article was first published in *Bloomberg View.*)

INDIA AND CHINA SHOULD LET TRADE DO THE TALKING

This article was first published in September 2014 just before the first meeting between Prime Minister Modi and Chinese President Xi Jinping. Since then, the two leaders have met several times as the India–China relationship has gone through periods of ups and serious downs (Doklam, for example). For historical reasons, the India–China relationship is complex, but its importance cannot be overstated as the two neighbours, also the two most populous countries in the world and the two fastest growing major economies of the world must find a way to engage constructively. Both sides need to focus much more on the positives that deeper economic engagement can bring. For now, India has a terribly skewed balance of trade with China which has grown dramatically since the early 2000s. This needs to be bridged in two ways. First, by expanding India's exports to China, particularly of services. Second, by attracting more Chinese direct investment in India. In order to do this, both sides will need to abandon old paranoias. The power of economic integration can ultimately transform the bilateral relationship between India and China.

Relations between China and India—the world's two most populous countries, neighbours and rivals—have long been prickly. A lot depends on the personalities of the two leaders and the relationship between them. On paper, China's President Xi Jinping, and the Indian Prime Minister Narendra Modi, have much in common.

While Xi is China's first leader born after the 1949 revolution, Modi is India's first prime minister born after Independence in 1947. They represent not just generational but substantive change, having staked their credibility on enacting huge, difficult reforms. Both boast an enviable amount of political capital at home.

No matter how well they get along, there's little chance the two men will solve the decades-old border dispute that led their nations into war in 1962. Instead they should focus their efforts where a little political will could make a real difference: the sixty-five billion US dollars in bilateral trade between them.

Even given the fact that China is the more dominant economic power, the trade relationship with India is badly skewed. India's trade deficit with China has grown steadily from less than one billion dollars in 2000–01 to 36.2 billion dollars in 2013–14. That accounts for a full quarter of India's total trade deficit.

China's contribution to financing that deficit is negligible. Its total investment in India between 2000–2014 is in the range of just 400 million dollars. And the annual figure has been declining—from eighty-eight million in 2008 to just twenty-seven million dollars in 2013. By comparison, China invested fourteen *billion* dollars in the US that same year.

One reason for the yawning trade deficit is that a majority of China's exports to India are manufactured goods, while most of India's exports to China are primary goods such as, iron ore and other minerals, which have little value added. That isn't necessarily surprising. China has a strong manufacturing base and India does not.

At the same time, though, India has legitimate concerns about Chinese non-tariff barriers that block market access for goods in which India has a comparative advantage such as, pharmaceuticals and meat. Similar obstacles confront the Indian services industry. Tough visa rules, for instance, make it harder for IT professionals to execute service contracts on the mainland. India's entertainment industry, particularly television, has had trouble penetrating a lucrative market which is a surprisingly big consumer of Indian soap operas. In 2012, Zee TV became the first Indian channel to be granted broadcast rights in China, after a six-year wait. Both countries would stand to gain if China lowered such barriers.

To spur investment, India needs to clear its own roadblocks. Paranoia about Chinese spying has unnecessarily complicated greater Chinese investment in India's telecoms sector, as Huawei and ZTE have discovered in recent years. Despite a desperate need to improve power and roads—sectors where Chinese money and expertise should be welcome—India continues to limit the import of Chinese labour.

Just as importantly, deeper economic engagement could help cool geopolitical tensions. While the European Union hasn't exactly been a role model for effective multilateral cooperation in recent years, it continues to illustrate how deep economic integration can make borders less relevant. If they can get trade and investment conditions right, Modi and Xi should find more intractable challenges easier to solve.

(This article was first published in *Bloomberg View.*)

INDIA'S ASIAN INTEGRATION STRATEGY

The region of South Asia is one of the least advanced in the global economy. Unsurprisingly, it is also one of the least integrated. This article published in 2016 argues that more efforts are needed to create a common market in South Asia if prosperity is to be achieved in rapid time.

The Indian economy is experiencing rapid growth of between seven–eight per cent a year. To sustain that growth rate and for India to achieve its development potential, it must open up its economy and have a strong export sector. It may not be easy, but given the global trade slowdown and the paralysis of multilateral trade negotiations, India's best bet is to seize those opportunities for integration closest to home.

Thanks to its strength in the service sector, India's trade to GDP ratio is around twenty-five per cent, close to that of China or Indonesia. But in terms of merchandise trade, India simply does not match up to the region's other big players, accounting for just 1.7 per cent of global merchandise exports. In comparison, the United States accounts for nine per cent, the European Union for 13.5 per cent and China for fourteen per cent.

Unlike its East Asian neighbours, India is in a region

characterised by remarkably little intraregional trade. Just five per cent of South Asian trade takes place within the region, compared to twenty-five per cent for ASEAN or fifty-five per cent for Asia as a whole. What are the roadblocks to greater economic integration with India's neighbours, dynamic East Asia and the global economy? And what can be done?

Some ingrained domestic opposition to openness can be explained by historical factors. Socialist development policies and import substitution industrialisation strategies are within living memory for many in India. Then there are contemporary obstacles. India trades less than its East Asian neighbours in part because its manufacturing and agricultural sectors are relatively less competitive, and in part because of its big domestic market. The dynamics of liberalisation are also a factor—opening up to trade usually leads to a sharper rise in imports than exports in the short run.

What's more, trade agreements tend to mainly affect goods, with less attention paid to services, India's most competitive sector. Services are particularly vulnerable in international markets to non-tariff barriers like visas or complex regulatory requirements.

For India, the path towards economic integration begins at home. The implementation of the historic Goods and Services Tax has created a single market within India. Yet as it stands, the GST requires critical reform. Forty per cent of India's indirect taxes come from oil, tobacco and alcohol. These industries will remain outside the federal GST and in the hands of the country's twenty-nine states.

Since the early 1990s, India's economy has risen on the strength of services while manufacturing has declined. This emphasis is now changing in policy debate. The government's flagship Make in India initiative—a suite of proposed reforms aimed at boosting the competitiveness of Indian manufacturing—must follow through on the policy vision it offers. India needs a strong manufacturing sector because of the size of its low-skilled population and high demand for jobs. At present, manufacturing firms migrating out of China are more likely to set up shop in Southeast Asia than India.

Improving ease of doing business is a worthy policy priority that is receiving growing attention as part of the Make in India initiative. Making it quicker and easier to register a business, cutting red tape and simplifying the tax return process are areas flagged for reform. Following a public commitment by the prime minister, the Department of Industrial Policy and Promotion announced in late 2016 that it wants to see India reach the global top fifty in the World Bank's Ease of Doing Business index.

India's infrastructure potential is all too often limited by bureaucratic bloat. Major ports are causing shippers frustration as smaller, private ports increase their efficiency and market share. Railways charge firms more in order to cross-subsidise fares for passengers, an arrangement which has long affected competitiveness. That means more goods are transported by road, the efficiency of which is marred by state-specific taxes and poor road quality. The good news is that the current government is approaching infrastructure upgrading with renewed focus.

One promising strategy is the use of 'coastal employment zones' in the style of the Special Economic Zones in Shenzhen and Guangdong, China. By introducing flexible land and labour rules in limited areas, rather than to the country as a whole, these could provide a politically viable solution for overcoming the highly restrictive impact of these laws on business. Over the medium term, the zones are aimed at attracting large manufacturing firms that exit China as wages there rise.

But the strategy wouldn't be easy to implement. Coastal land is hard to acquire, and unlike China, India is a federalist democracy. A policy that works in a Special Economic Zone can't be quickly rolled out across the country as was so successfully done in China.

When it comes to trade, China is still the elephant in India's room. India's trade deficit with China is substantial and rising—53 billion US dollars in 2015–16 compared to less than one billion in 2000–01. China's non-tariff barriers on sectors like entertainment, Information Technology, pharmaceuticals and meat hit India particularly hard in the areas where it's most competitive.

On top of this, China's investment in India is relatively small, especially for a large neighbour. India was the destination for just 240 million US dollars of China's outbound investment in 2013—less than many of China's smaller neighbours, like Kazakhstan (1.34 billion), Vietnam (790 million), Myanmar (780 million), and Pakistan (270 million).

The SAARC countries—India, Afghanistan, Bangladesh, Bhutan, Nepal, Pakistan, the Maldives and Sri Lanka—form one of the least economically integrated regions in the world. This remains the case despite the South Asian Free Trade Area (SAFTA) having come into force in 2006.

SAFTA has been hobbled by political tensions between India and Pakistan, its two largest members. Pakistan refuses to grant India most-favoured nation status, though India granted it to Pakistan in 1996. Given recent trends, it's unlikely that SAARC or SAFTA will be the foundation for greater economic integration for India.

India's sub-regional arrangements are more promising for integration. The BBIN initiative provides a framework for these four countries to coordinate on trade, connectivity and management of resources. In 2015, BBIN members signed a motor vehicle agreement to allow vehicles carrying export goods to cross borders without having to trans-ship the goods to a separate vehicle in the importing country. This is a fundamental condition for cross-border trade.

Another sub-regional arrangement, BIMSTEC—the Bay of Bengal Initiative for Multi-sectoral Technical and Economic Co-operation—has been getting renewed thrust in recent years as an economic bridge between South and Southeast Asia.

ASEAN presents improving prospects for Indian economic integration. The India–ASEAN free trade agreement, which came into effect in 2010, resulted in a substantial two-way trade growth for India. Southeast Asia borders India's least developed states, posing opportunities for the country's relatively poorer east and northeast.

ASEAN remains India's best option for integrating with 'global value chains'—the constantly expanding production networks that are at the heart of international trade in the twenty-first century and in which services play a crucial role. Its headline initiative, the Regional Comprehensive Economic Partnership (RCEP) is a 'comprehensive' opportunity. India has warmed up to RCEP recently, dropping its insistence on a three-tier tariff concession structure, though it remains the most obstructionist member of the agreement. Navigating around the political distance with China will remain the key challenge for India's trade negotiators.

Double-digit growth is only possible for India with a strong export sector. The pace of global trade growth is slowing, multilateral trade negotiations through the World Trade Organisation are at a dead end, and the Trans-Pacific Partnership is a thing of the past. If India moves too slowly on trade, it will miss the bus; if it moves too fast, it could suffer a domestic backlash.

Engaging more deeply with the rest of Asia—especially through ASEAN-led and sub-regional initiatives—is India's best option.

(This article was first published in the *East Asia Forum*.)

BAD ECONOMICS, MR GANDHI

This article was first published in October 2011 when Rahul Gandhi, the then 'heir-apparent' to the Congress presidency made one of his rare substantive speeches on policy. Mr Gandhi's reflexively anti-free market stance was reflective of an outdated ideology and not in sync with the reality of the world and indeed the reality of India twenty years after liberalisation. The argument remains valid seven years on as Mr Gandhi positions himself as a potential prime minister. To capture popular imagination, he needs to have a more modernising view of economic policy. Markets are not anti-poor. In fact, they work well for the poor as the tremendous success of a private sector-led telecom revolution has shown.

Rahul Gandhi's introductory address at a public lecture to celebrate the twentieth anniversary of the Rajiv Gandhi Institute of Contemporary Studies on 18 October 2011 provided a rare insight into the Congress heir's worldview. It also laid bare the Congress party's continued, and damaging, ambivalence on economic policy. Making perhaps his most definitive statement on economic policy, Rahul said, 'Globalisation excludes as much as it includes. There are millions left out of the process, millions who do not benefit from globalisation.' The clear emphasis was on those left out, a kosher Left-of-Centre stance. That worldview would have fit in well with Indira Gandhi's pro-poor Congress party. It may, however, be out of sync with history in 2011. It is the time for India to embrace globalisation more strongly than ever before.

More than thirty years after this wave of globalisation was unleashed by the Reagan–Thatcher revolution in the early 1980s, the advanced economies—the US, Europe and Japan—are in serious, if not terminal decline. The global balance of economic power is shifting towards the emerging economies—India, China, Brazil, Russia and South Africa. Investors earning meagre returns in the West are looking to move elsewhere. China and India, as the two largest and fastest growing emerging economies, are the obvious beneficiaries. Rahul Gandhi is absolutely right when he warns that India's success is not inevitable. However, the most serious obstacle to India's success would not be globalisation, but an old-fashioned, confused and uncertain Congress party ruling at the Centre.

Modern parties of the Centre-Left, which have reinvented themselves over two decades across the world, view free markets and globalisation as a largely positive force. The way to address exclusion is not to block globalisation, but to use calibrated intervention to ensure greater inclusion. The Congress party's basic instincts have been to block the forces of globalisation as was evident in the UPA government's refusal to allow greater FDI in retail, insurance, aviation among other sectors, even without the chains of the Left that shackled it in UPA-I. In a different sphere, the government, in collaboration with the RBI, did nothing to liberalise India's financial system which means that the average Indian consumer or business paid significantly more interest on a loan than his counterpart elsewhere. The exclusion of millions of Indians from access to cheap finance is a failure of government, not free markets.

The logic of globalisation is that it should benefit even the less skilled in India. Global manufacturing is constantly looking for cheap labour. Unfortunately, India's restrictive labour laws send global manufacturers to China depriving millions of poor Indians of a factory job. That is a failure of government. That there are not enough Indians with the education to get high-skilled jobs created by globalisation is also a failure of the government—its failure to evolve better delivery systems for public goods like education and health. It is convenient for politicians like Rahul Gandhi to blame the faceless forces of the free market and globalisation for the poverty of India's millions. It would be more fruitful if the young Mr Gandhi was to reinvent his party's archaic thinking on economics.

(This article was first published in *India Today*.)

FREE MARKET, LAST GANDHI

This article was first published in December 2011 at a time when the UPA government was getting bogged down by allegations of corruption and economic mismanagement. This was also the time when the government dithered on a major reform, permitting foreign investment in retail, purportedly because of the opposition of the Trinamool Congress. The article argues that Rahul Gandhi and the Congress party were equally reluctant about a market reform such as this because the essence of free markets is the anti-thesis of the politics of dynasty. Free markets are about merit and hard work. Dynastic politics is feudal. The article urges Rahul Gandhi to embrace the meritocracy of the market to change his party's fortunes. That argument remains valid and perhaps more urgent, seven years on.

The Congress party has a new fig leaf for its bare naked opposition to free market reform. Mamata Banerjee's Trinamool Congress is as allergic to the free market as the Communists whom she replaced in government in West Bengal in 2011. It was bound to oppose foreign investment in retail. The truth is that the economic policy DNA of the Congress isn't radically different from either Mamata or the Communists.

The genes of the Congress descend from its first family.

Neither Sonia Gandhi, nor the President, Rahul Gandhi uttered a word to support foreign investment in retail. That they allowed, in steely silence, the public spectacle of a humiliating surrender by the government is sufficient indication of their real view on foreign investment in retail. The reason why the mother–son duo never supported economic reform in public, is because the economics of the free market is an antithesis of the politics of inheritance. The free market brings with it the principle of merit and the importance of individual, self-made achievement. The Indian State, mired in the politics of populism, has never had any regard for merit, even less for talent. It has usually thrived on lineage, connections and narrow parochial politics.

However, twenty and more years of economic reforms have begun to change that. There is now a significant middle class of people whose success has nothing to do with the patronage of the State. In fact, it is directly related to the State reducing its role in economic activity. Twenty more years of economic liberalisation will demolish the entire old edifice. The entrenched establishment will lose out and particularly the dynasty that has headed the Congress for six decades.

The Gandhis do not engage with the new meritocratic India. They prefer to talk to India's poor. Patronising the poor with government freebies, in return for votes, has been for years the cornerstone of their political strategy. In 2014, and in the subsequent assembly elections thereafter, including in Uttar Pradesh and Gujarat, that strategy came a cropper because the poor marginalised saw through what was clearly a vote-garnering plan by India's oldest party, which had little or nothing to do with economic progress. Unfortunately, in the long term, that strategy can only succeed if significant number of Indians remain mired in poverty. Two decades of double-digit economic growth, which will happen only with market-oriented reform, could make the poor a very small minority, not enough to win elections. Rahul could begin talking to the prosperous. But those who have achieved success the hard way would have scant regard for someone who has claimed India's party of freedom as his inheritance. Some of this was evident in the Anna Hazare-led movement against corruption earlier in 2011 when the educated youth in urban India chose to heed the leadership of a seventy-three-year-old Gandhian rather than the forty-one-year-old Gandhi.

Amongst several other things, Rahul often talks about the need for more democracy and merit in the Congress. Those are empty words as long as he protects the status quo on top. At the very least, he should make every effort to unshackle India from the discredited politics of populism and patronage. A prosperous India will inevitably reject political dynasties. Rahul may well be the last Gandhi to lead the Congress. Does he have the good sense to be on the right side of history?

(This article was first published in *India Today*.)

WHAT NEXT FOR GLOBALISATION?

This article was first published recently, in 2017, as the backlash against globalisation and free markets captured popular imagination in the advanced economies. This article argues that the backlash against globalisation and free markets will be damaging to prosperity and that India and other emerging economies must take leadership in preserving the forces that drive globalisation.

When the economic history of our times is eventually written, the year 2016 will occupy a prominent place. It will be remembered as the year in which the two countries that had laid the foundation for globalisation, free markets and prosperity in the early 1980s, switched course and chose to hit the stop button (a long pause if you are an optimist). It was the leadership of Ronald Reagan in the US, and Margaret Thatcher in the UK, which unleashed the forces of the free market within their countries and the forces of integration and openness elsewhere. It is with considerable irony that historians will note the fact that in both countries, the long pause on globalisation was hit by leaders of the political parties of Reagan and Thatcher. It was the supposedly Right-wing, free market Republicans in the US led by Donald Trump, and a faction of the Brexit Conservatives in the UK led by Boris Johnson, who led the charge for closing the doors. What was started by politicians on the Right of the political spectrum, has been stopped by the politicians on the same side, surely a rare occurrence in the history of politics.

The triumph of the politics of anti-integration over the economics of globalisation portends danger for the global economy, particularly its poorest citizens. At no point in history have so many hundreds of millions of people been lifted out of poverty than in the last three decades. This is obviously attributable to the rapid growth of China and India, where the maximum number of people (and the maximum number of poor people resided), but also the growth of Africa and the former Communist countries of Eastern Europe. Now, the economic openness of the world economy on the basis of which these countries have liberalised their own economies and alleviated poverty is under question. Going forward, there are reasons for pessimism, reasons for optimism and plenty of reason for introspection.

Consider the state of the economies of the major nations when Reagan and Thatcher got started. The US and West Europe were suffering from stagnating growth and high inflation; the USSR and East Europe were ever closer to bankruptcy; Africa and Latin America were near basket cases; China was just about taking its first steps to overcome its economic isolation and near ruin; India and South Asia were cocooned in poverty; only Japan and the East Asian Tiger economies had signs of economic dynamism. In a period of twenty-five years, circa 2006–07, after a sustained period of market reforms, the situation was dramatically different; the US and Europe were in a boom (the latter having moved to even closer integration via a single currency); the USSR was long dead, Russia had achieved a reasonable equilibrium after chaos, and East Europe was on the fast track to growth; Africa and much of Latin America had long overcome the stagnation of the 1970s and 1980s; China was in the reckoning for global superpower; India had woken from its long economic slumber and growing at near double-digits; the rest of South Asia was not far behind; and East Asia continued to be dynamic. It seemed that stagnating Japan was the only dull spot in the globalised economy.

That was until September 2008 when the spectacular collapse of Lehman Brothers and the subsequent near collapse of the global financial system changed the narrative. There were obvious questions in the US and UK (also Europe) about whether the free market revolution had gone too far too fast without adequate regulatory oversight. But the legitimacy of global capitalism began to be questioned a couple of years later when it became apparent that government bailouts of large banks and finance companies—presented as a necessity for a recovery of growth—had led to very limited changes in the practices, executive pay and risk-taking behaviour of global finance. At the same time, governments, which had financed large bailouts of the private sector, came under acute fiscal stress, triggering a second phase of the crisis in 2010–11 when a set of countries in southern Europe (referred to disparagingly as the PIGS) faced serious sovereign debt crises.

Ironically enough, the backlash against what was a crisis, essentially triggered by global finance and exacerbated by overspending governments, ended up targetting the free movement of goods (open trade) and the free movements of people (liberal immigration policies)—a combination of both in the US and the latter in the UK. And to add to the irony, a crisis in capitalism was exploited not by parties on the Left of the political spectrum, but on the hard Right. Free trade and immigration provided relatively soft, and easily identifiable targets compared with the elite, in the shadowy world of global finance. The fact that technological change and increased automation in both manufacturing and services were reducing jobs, and depressing wages all along, was often overlooked as more spectacular and visible shocks to the economies of the advanced West hit home.

Unfortunately, for the world as a whole, the trends for the near term do not suggest any immediate reversion to openness. There are three clear adverse trends to note. First, the advanced economies of the West, potentially beyond the US and UK, are set to increasingly look inward. On immigration, almost every advanced country will erect more barriers as political formations of the hard Right gain ascendancy. The rise of the hard Right will force the conventional Right to take stronger anti-immigration positions. The appetite for opening up trade has already reduced—the WTO is stagnant, the much-hyped Trans Pacific Partnership is virtually dead—even if the real causes for job losses lie elsewhere. Second, automation (and Artificial Intelligence) is proceeding at a remarkable speed posing a complex challenge for most economies, even emerging economies like China and India. A recent World Bank study concluded that automation threatens sixty-nine per cent of existing jobs in India, and seventy-seven per cent of existing jobs in China. If the predictions begin to materialise, it will put countries on the defensive in terms of economic policy, never mind the fact that any jobs that are lost may be compensated by other jobs that are created. It is only realistic to note that any such transition would create losers in the short run—and politics is about the short term—and would require a different type of skill in the workforce. The third trend has little to do with economics, but it will impact the global economy adversely. And that is the spectre of Islamic terrorism which has now engulfed a wide geography from India's Western frontiers to Europe's Eastern and Southern frontiers (with parts of East Asia forming fertile ground). The trend of Islamic extremism is unlikely to ebb anytime soon, particularly if it has powerful backers in the form of countries like Saudi Arabia and Pakistan. And the longer it creates terror, the stronger will be the backlash against openness (particularly to immigration) in general.

It isn't all despair. Historically, every time the world has gone through a cycle of inwardness/autarky, islands of openness have shone bright. Consider how the tiger economies and the newly-industrialising countries of East Asia industrialised rapidly with pro-market, export-oriented trade strategies between the 1960s and 1980s when the global economy was hardly at its most open or integrated. The countries of Western Europe also gained from economic integration via the EEC and EU through the 1970s. In an earlier era, in the early twentieth century, the United States of America used open, pro-market policies to prosper just as Europe was miring itself in war.

Now, there is an opportunity for India and the rest of emerging Asia (geographically to India's East) to don the mantle and make the most of openness. India, in particular, has a lot to gain by looking outward. Even in a slowing global trade environment, there is an eighteen trillion US dollars global market in merchandise trade of which India has only a 1.7 per cent share. China has almost fourteen per cent, around the same as EU and a little more than the US. India can still achieve greater prosperity by using exports as an engine of growth. Fortunately, the trends in automation suggest that the jobs which will be affected first are in a high to medium technology industries. It will take longer for automation to be commercially viable in labour-intensive industries where India ought to have a big comparative advantage and where China is losing its advantage because of a rise in wages. This opportunity applies not just to India, but other emerging economies in Asia like Bangladesh, Vietnam, Indonesia, Cambodia, and the Philippines. To take full advantage of the opportunity, India and others must remain open to foreign trade and foreign investment. It is unrealistic to believe that just domestic firms and domestic markets (no matter how big) will be sufficient to drive the kind of growth emerging Asia needs. Equally, it is critical to put the house in order and create enabling conditions for such investment and trade, primarily by building world-class infrastructure but also by reforming labour and land laws.

Of course, India and other emerging economies in Asia can learn from the excesses of the capitalist system in the advanced economies and follow a different approach to financial markets liberalisation for instance. That doesn't mean keeping systems closed, but evolving the right kind of regulation that is able to limit risks. On safety nets, emerging economies can learn from the failures of the West and reorient their strategies. For instance, rather than fiscally unsustainable and labour market-distorting doles, there can be a greater emphasis on skilling and reskilling, the only guarantors of jobs in a technology-intensive world.

The triumph of the politics of fear and the economics of inwardness in some of the most prosperous regions of the world needs to be challenged. It is a formidable task for political parties and thinkers on the Left, Centre-Left and Centre-Right of the political spectrum in the advanced countries. The bad news for the Left is that it does not seem to have succeeded in presenting a credible alternative to voters despite the obvious crises in the current system. In the UK, for instance, Labour's move further to the Left under the leadership of Jeremy

Corbyn has only further marginalised its appeal. In France, the forthcoming election battle is predicted to be between the hard Right and Right. Even in emerging economies, the Left is in a lurch. The Chinese Communist Party abandoned ideology long ago. The populist Left in Latin America has come a cropper, most spectacularly in Venezuela. In India, the Left parties are less relevant than ever before and parties on the Centre-Left like the Congress have lost credibility with voters. The Left has a real problem. In its zealousness for an ever greater role for the State in economic matters, it overlooks a historical fact—a heavy hand of the State is usually associated with corruption, rent-seeking, inefficiency, stagnation and inequality, none of which appeal to voters.

That said, there is room for modern Centre-Left and Centre-Right parties to reclaim lost ground. It is absolutely reasonable to have a contest of ideas and a contest in politics between varying roles for the State in a system which is fundamentally governed by efficient free markets. Smart regulation, for instance, is critical to the proper functioning of markets. Functioning safety nets are required for those who lose out in transitions. The problem is that many mainstream political parties, particularly in the advanced economies, on the Centre-Left and Centre-Right were lulled into a sense of complacency by the apparently unending prosperity of the 1980s, 1990s and 2000s. They failed to see the disaffection (on inequality, on stagnant wages, on joblessness) simmering under the surface. There was a cosy consensus in the mainstream, which was bound to be shattered.

Needless to say, grievances of the people need to be addressed in any democratic system (perhaps even in autocracies as the Arab Spring showed) but they should not require a lurch to the hard Right or hard Left, both of which are forces against prosperity.

Perhaps the emerging economies of South and East Asia can lead by example and show that a richer and more equitable world is possible while retaining openness and shunning extreme ideologies. It's time for a new Asian Consensus. The world needs it to preserve and enhance prosperity.

(This article was first published in the *Economic and Political Weekly*.)

TAX HAVENS POSE GRAVE THREAT TO LEGITIMACY OF GLOBAL CAPITALISM

In many emerging economies, including India, the greatest damage to the cause of capitalism is done by capitalists. This article was written in November 2017 at the time when the Panama Papers leak made global headlines. For a market economy to have legitimacy, all actors must be seen to be playing by the rules of the game. In particular, it is expected that taxes are paid fairly since the tax system is the most efficient way of redistribution. Modi's government has been very conscious of the threat that tax evasion and black money pose to the legitimacy of India's still evolving market economy and have taken several actions to curb the menace.

There is trouble in paradise. A new leak has reignited the unpleasant spectre of tax havens in popular imagination. Not all that has been revealed in the 'Paradise Papers' is illegal. There is a difference between tax evasion, which involves breaking the law, and tax avoidance, which merely finds loopholes.

Tax evaders can be punished, not tax avoiders. But even if no law is broken, tax havens pose a serious challenge to the legitimacy of the global capitalist order. The world need not worry just yet about the tiny minority of romantics celebrating a hundred years of the Russian Revolution in November 2017.

But it would be foolhardy to be blind to the crisis of legitimacy for the global market economy. Warts and all, it is still the best system we have.

Interestingly, in the advanced economies, the protracted slowdown post-2008 financial crisis has led to a backlash by workers against workers. The surge of Right-wing populism against the mainstream parties of both the Left and Right, which ruled most Western democracies in the boom decades of the 1980s, 1990s and 2000s, has ridden on the shoulders of the middle class and working class who are angry in their perception of jobs lost to workers in China (in manufacturing) or India (in services).

It is the failure of mainstream parties that they have failed to recognise either real grievances or been able to highlight the successes of the boom years, most notably in the form of cheaper goods and services to consumers. That they turned a blind eye to the most egregious side of globalisation—the failure to penalise the perpetrators of the 2008 crisis in the world of global finance—further fuelled anger.

The Left failed to bring to the fore the clearly emerging unfairness in the global economy: not the tired cry of the rich getting richer but, instead, the fact that the wealthy were enriching themselves at the expense of State—and taxpayer-funded bailouts and then stashing away money in tax havens.

For romantics of the Revolution, the inequality inherent in a capitalist system is reason enough for its downfall. That is a faulty assumption. People do not necessarily grudge others their wealth if it is fairly earned (and taxes paid). But they will grudge inequality that is exacerbated by cronyism and tax evasion or avoidance.

So far, politics in the West has channelled the anger of

citizens to the immigrant or foreign worker. That will only damage the global economy, which functions efficiently because goods, services and people move borders. Autarky, as the late Soviet Union showed, is a more calamitous policy than any other. Instead, the anger ought to be channelled towards the tax avoidance and tax evasion of the wealthy, which prevents the tax system from acting as a natural redistributor of wealth.

In India, too, there is a backlash against the cronyism and tax evasion that characterised the boom years between 1991 and 2012. Fortunately, the anger was not channelled at trade or openness, but at the nexus between business and politics. A drastic clean-up of the system, whether through demonetisation, or a tough bankruptcy law or a transparent Goods and Services Tax, was absolutely necessary to allow the market economy to function again.

The task is enormous. On tax evasion and tax avoidance, India is way ahead of advanced countries. India's tax GDP ratio of seventeen per cent of GDP is just half the OECD average. For an emerging economy, which needs to invest in its poorest citizens, taxes must be paid. While each country, including India, can do its bit to crack down on tax evasion and tax avoidance at home, no single country can tackle the challenge posed by tax havens by itself. Given that the crisis of legitimacy of the market economy is now quite widely spread, it is imperative that a forum like the G20 put the agenda of tax avoidance and tax havens right at the top.

Capitalism needs to rediscover its moral dimension. Of course, it would help if countries, including India, stuck to moderate tax rates to disincentive evasion and avoidance. But in the end, the global community of nations needs to agree on some rules. Apart from G20, other international institutions like the OECD, the World Bank, the International Monetary Fund (IMF), the Asian Infrastructure Investment Bank (AIIB), and the New Development Bank can concentrate their minds on how to ensure fairness in the payment of taxes.

The world's wealthy should also have an interest in cooperating. After all, it is the functioning market economy that has enabled them to generate wealth. The last thing either India or any other country would want is a popular revolt against the idea of wealth. The unprecedented prosperity achieved in the last four decades in both advanced and emerging economies would then be at threat. It may cheer the Bolsheviks, but it would bring greater misery to the world.

(This article was first published in *The Economic Times*.)

NATION AND AUTOMATION

This article was first published in February 2017 at a time when global policy discourse had begun taking note of the arrival of the fourth industrial revolution. The discourse usually centres on the potential of job losses as machines begin to replace humans in key tasks. This article presents a counter-intuitive view on why the fourth industrial revolution may actually present a unique opportunity for India to leapfrog to prosperity. But only if the country trusts market forces.

Once upon a time an economic heavyweight, India has a long—two-and-a-half century old—habit of missing the bus of the most tectonic, prosperity-enhancing, shifts in the global economy. When the first Industrial Revolution swept through Europe in the late eighteenth and early nineteenth centuries, mechanising the textile industry and unleashing the power of the steam engine, India was experiencing the slow demise of the Mughal empire and the gradual emergence of a British empire, neither of which would prepare it to join the bandwagon of prosperity. At the time of the second industrial revolution at the beginning of the twentieth century, characterised by a move to mass production and electric power, India was a colony (with no economic autonomy) on the verge of a mass movement against the Empire. When the third industrial revolution dawned in the

1980s, with the advent of modern PCs, the internet and digital technologies, India was in the last throes of socialism, a system which had over four decades denied it a chance to 'catch up' with leaders of the second industrial revolution, something countries in East Asia, like Korea, Taiwan and Singapore achieved and others like China, Malaysia and Thailand made significant strides in doing. Unsurprisingly, an over-protected India failed to make the most of the new opportunities in manufacturing (mobile phones, PCs, laptops, other digital electronics) that came with these new technologies.

The world is on the cusp of a fourth industrial revolution. Will India be at the station when the bus rolls in? Or is it destined to play catch up?

It is a fraught exercise to predict the future; only astrologers and economists hazard it. For nations, just like for individuals, there is a link between the past and the future, perhaps even a path dependency. There are some things we know well from India's experience with the second and third industrial revolutions. First, the country has never excelled at manufacturing, not even to a level that the erstwhile Soviet Union achieved before its collapse. Second, the government has always believed that it knows the answers to the most vexed challenges, but invariably its interventions have been counter-productive, too intrusive in spheres where unnecessary (think labour laws, high taxes, the erstwhile licence raj) and too little in spheres which needed it most (think infrastructure). Third, India has remarkably managed to achieve a reasonable degree of progress and rate of growth, particularly in the last quarter of a century, despite those limitations, primarily driven by the services sector and entrepreneurs of outstanding talent. All of this is very relevant to India's future economic trajectory.

The fourth industrial revolution will be about a serious intensification of the trends seen in the third industrial revolution. We are talking about Artificial Intelligence, robots, automation, and 3D printing. In the end, whenever it materialises, whether in a decade or two from now, it will alter the world economy and indeed society in a way that the first Industrial Revolution did—at the roots, in the core. A lot of the commentary around the fourth industrial revolution centres on the exciting technology that would usher it in, but plenty also focuses on the potential job losses in all economies as a result of those technological breakthroughs. While it is true that many jobs as we know them today will be destroyed, there will be many new jobs that we may not know of today that will be created. Each industrial revolution is about creative destruction: old jobs and industries die, others rise. The trouble is that the new isn't a like-for-like replacement of the old; hence those who found productive employment in the old order may not find it easily in the new order.

Elements of the forthcoming industrial revolution are already on display, most noticeably the rise in automation in different sectors. High-tech industries like aerospace engineering are already highly automated. But changes are happening elsewhere in the value chain. Speed factory, the all new automated robot-operated factory in Germany by Adidas, for example, is experimenting to replace a traditional labour-intensive activity by machines. Ultimately, the application of automation and Artificial Intelligence in real-world activities depends on the cost economics. In advanced countries like Germany, where labour is scarce and expensive, it may be worth replacing people with machines. In developing and emerging economies like India, given the lower costs of human resources, the economics may not favour machines yet. The fourth industrial revolution will be upon us when machines can operate at a scale and at a cost economical enough to replace human resources across the board even in countries like India. There is some time to go for that to happen.

But, already, it is clear that the opportunities for low-skilled, skilled, semi-educated workers who traditionally find employment in labour-intensive industries may not exist in the near future. This may not be as bad for India as it sounds, largely because India has failed to create factory jobs on a mass scale that China and other East Asian countries did or the US and Europe did before them.

If there's one metric on which India's economic performance has underwhelmed, even in periods of impressive growth, it is in the generation of jobs in the quantum necessary to productively employ the country's workforce. The best statistic to sum it up is the one which tells that almost fifty per cent of India's workforce is still employed in agriculture, producing just fourteen per cent of total GDP. According to the theory of development economics, it is industry or manufacturing which performs the task of absorbing the excess workforce that exists in agriculture. And that is what has been seen in practice in much of East Asia and China as those economies have advanced. India has defied conventional wisdom. The share of industry in GDP and the share of manufacturing in employment has barely grown in the last twenty-five years since India liberalised its economy and grew rapidly, touching near double-digits in the 2000s. Unlike in other emerging economies, the services sector has created more decent quality jobs in comparison to manufacturing.

The most prominent of India's vast services sector industry is Information Technology. It is the one services industry where India has produced world-class companies which operate on a global scale and which has created millions of jobs for India's educated middle-class. However, it isn't infotech services alone, which has created well-paid jobs. Less glamorous sectors like hotels and restaurants and real estate have generated millions of jobs for those at the bottom end of the skill spectrum, absorbing at least some of the labour force exiting agriculture.

Development economists have been sceptical about a services-led strategy for catch up, emphasising a manufacturing-led strategy instead. They have good reasons for that. For one, every country that has advanced in the course of history since the industrial revolution, has developed a strong manufacturing base before moving to a more service-oriented economy once high income status has been achieved. Also, services were not traditionally seen as being able to generate export earnings since a large number of them were not tradeable. And, in general, the potential for productivity growth in manufacturing outstripped services.

India may yet defy the conventional wisdom. In many ways, it already has, growing rapidly without a strong labour-intensive manufacturing base. But the nature of services has changed. Infotech services, for example, are highly exportable. Services like education and health have tremendous potential to earn foreign exchange through medical tourism and people abroad seeking educational opportunities in India. India has performed woefully in attracting tourists when tourism is one of the most labour-intensive and potentially foreign exchange earning sectors of the economy. Needless to say, India's potential for tourism of all kinds—heritage, nature, adventure—is huge.

What is more significant, looking into the future, is the fact that automation is less likely to take over some of the labour-intensive services sectors— such as tourism—than manufacturing.

India definitely has a services-advantage. And it could be argued that the manufacturing-first pathway that worked for Europe or East Asia may not work for India, especially if commercially viable automation and Artificial Intelligence arrive in the next decade. On the other hand, the line between manufacturing and services may blur as technology evolves.

Consider a product like Apple's iPhone. The real value added is not so much in the manufacturing part which happens in China, but in the design and innovation part (which could also qualify as services) which happens in the US. In the final analysis, it is perhaps best, therefore, to be agnostic about which sector of the economy will lead growth and development.

There are two big trends—one positive and one negative—that policymakers and other stakeholders should hold on to tightly as the future unravels. The good news first. India's limited global success stories have come in knowledge-intensive industries. Apart from infotech, India has built a globally competitive generic pharmaceuticals industry, and a reasonably robust automobile engineering industry. In what is an exception more than the rule, India's space programme has done remarkably well despite being under government control. Autonomy in operations and distance from Delhi may have helped Indian Space Research Organisation or ISRO achieve what other public organisations have not. In short, India has already shown the ability to leapfrog the traditional path of labour-intensive manufacturing to high-tech manufacturing and services. This is a positive trend as the world heads towards an ever greater knowledge-based economy. Just like the setting up of the IITs and Indian Institute of Science (IIS) shortly after Independence laid the foundation for India's infotech boom decades later, a strong foundation of knowledge industries will yield high returns in a world driven more and more by technology in a decade or two from now.

Second is the role performed by the government, which has been negative on balance even in recent decades. Despite the steps taken to liberalise the economy over the last two decades and more, India's State apparatus hasn't given up its tendency to dabble in economic activity where unnecessary (via public sector businesses or over-regulation) and to be absent, or present in a most inefficient fashion, in areas where its role is necessary: in building, or at least financing, physical and social infrastructure. The big challenge for India is to move beyond islands of excellence to a general prosperity for all. And there remains a role for the government in that.

The overarching goal of the Centre's economic policy should be only one: the promotion and unleashing of entrepreneurship. Governments do not do a good job of picking winners. It is impossible to say with certainty for any bureaucrat or politician whether manufacturing or services, or whether sector A or B will be the dominant force of the future. The job of discovering that is best left to risk-taking capitalists. But for that to happen, the government needs to clear the messy web of over-regulation that chokes enterprise at birth. What the government also needs to focus on is the hardware (roads, power, airports and so on), and software (education, health, skills) that will encourage entrepreneurship. The government also needs to be ready for periods of possible disruptions in certain industries and jobs. It needs to lay out a reasonable, affordable safety net and re-skilling programmes for those who are bound to be affected by major technological shifts.

There is nothing spectacular in any of this, but the Government in India needs to retreat decisively from the frontlines of the economy to focus on building its backbone. If it fails to lay the foundation, India will be ill-prepared to shake the hand of the fourth industrial revolution when it does arrive in force. It may then be very long before India gets another chance to board the bus of prosperity for all.

(This article was first published in the *Open* magazine.)

CONCLUSION

There is nothing to doubt in India's latent economic powerhouse potential. Equally, there is nothing inevitable about India's economic rise. India has certainly progressed from where it started in 1947, but the rate of change has lagged its peers, especially in East Asia. Now, India needs an urgent transformation before the global economy is altered by the gradually emerging contours of the fourth industrial revolution. No transformation happens overnight, and no transformation takes place in the absence of enabling conditions. Thus far, during Prime Minister Narendra Modi's term in office, a strong effort has been made to lay the foundations on which a transformation can happen. The work is not over, but it is well begun.

The argument for transformation under Prime Minister Modi can be broadly disaggregated into three heads—reorientation of government, war against cronyism and corruption, and a narrative in favour of markets. First, there has been a decisive recast of government itself. It has become more federal with real partnership between the Government of India, the governments of states, and local bodies. Perhaps the best outcomes of these partnerships will come in India's most backward, or to use a positive connotation, aspirational, 115 districts. Uniquely, this is one flagship programme of the Union Government which doesn't seek any funds. Instead, it seeks to improve the delivery of existing schemes and resources to lift outcomes in education, health, agriculture, financial inclusion, skills and basic infrastructure. In fact, an emphasis on monitoring implementation and measuring outcomes has brought speed to an otherwise lethargic government machinery. And the strategy to use Jan Dhan accounts, Aadhaar and mobile phones for direct benefit transfers have brought huge savings to the government. The effort to improve the functioning of government has been complemented by a drive to reduce the government's counterproductive role in the rise of the private sector. This has been characterised by improving the ease of doing business, liberalising foreign investment including in defence, and restarting the strategic disinvestment programme.

The case for free markets has rarely found salience in India's political economy despite the overwhelming evidence from both theory and practice that a market-led economy is the best pathway to prosperity. Long decades of a socialist-style economy have ingrained a deep suspicion of wealth. Capitalists have not always helped the argument in favour of markets since many notable ones have indulged in crony capitalism. Their misdeeds have sometimes overshadowed real successes, particularly from the IT sector, but also other sectors like, pharmaceuticals where direct interface with the government is minimal and where competition is global. The fact is that on the policy front, firm conviction has never driven the economic reform process. It is hard for politicians to make the case for the invisible hand, especially in a low income country, because it leads to the perception that the government is leaving the vulnerable to the uncontrollable forces of free markets. Economists learn about the virtues of free markets in *Economics 101* textbooks or courses. But efficiency in the allocation of resources doesn't make a convincing political argument. Political economists learn about the risks of excessive State intervention in the context of interest groups and rent-seeking. That literature may perhaps provide more fertile ground for an argument for less government and more markets in the Indian context.

Ultimately, a political argument, if it is to be popular, must be devoid of academic jargon. The transformative Chinese leader, Deng Xiaoping famously declared that it is glorious to be rich as he turned China away from Communism to capitalism. He explained the need to be agnostic about ideology in policymaking as long as it delivered outcomes when he said that it doesn't matter whether the cat is black or white, as long as it catches mice. Of course, it is much harder to make a similar case in a plural democracy like India where populist noises in the Opposition can match the volume of the argument made by the government. Market reform is quickly branded as pro-rich and allegations are made of suit-boot ki sarkar.

Narendra Modi is the first Indian leader who has not been shy of making an argument in favour of free markets. He campaigned on the slogan of 'Minimum Government, Maximum Governance'. He constantly makes the case for entrepreneurship, of creating an ecosystem where Indians become job-creators rather than job-seekers. He has emphasised on innovation, a start-up culture and competition, and spoken against protectionism at the international stage. The rhetoric in favour of markets has been backed by action.

The government has implemented two major reforms which are often under-appreciated in how revolutionary they are. The Goods and Services Tax has laid the platform for a single market within the Indian union. Until GST, politically united

India had more barriers to trade between its states than the politically not-united and fractious European Union. No country has implemented GST without a troublesome transition period. In India, the transition is complicated by the fact that too many businesses which simply did not pay tax now have to. But things will smoothen out. The other big-ticket reform is the Law and Code on Bankruptcy. India has done a reasonable job of easing entry barriers to markets, but no thought was given to orderly exit, a prerequisite for a functioning market economy. The new code has joined the dots on an unfinished part of the reform process. These two major reforms have been supplemented by a host of others, including cutting red tape, improving the ease of doing business, liberalising foreign investment, and creating an independent monetary policy framework to be administered by the RBI for stable inflation. The last of these is hugely significant because India's record of high growth under the previous government had been blotted by rampant inflation.

Politically, the case for markets will not succeed unless there is a visible effort to clamp down on crony capitalism which seemed to have become the dominant feature of India's post-liberalisation economy, circa 2014. The battle against cronyism was begun as soon as Prime Minister Modi assumed office. There were two distinct strategies, enforcement or the penal side, and the preventive side which sought to limit the avenues for cronyism.

On the preventive front, the government for example committed to auctioning of all natural resources, or by cutting red tape in its bid to create a better environment for doing business. The second is ongoing. There was also the process of redoing Double Taxation Avoidance agreements and Tax Information Exchange agreements with several countries so that it would become harder for tax evaders to park their money overseas. On the penal side, the Modi government's first act was to set up a Special Investigation Team (SIT) on black money. The Benami Properties Act is a bold move to curb the menace of black money being parked in real estate. The biggest disrupter in the war against cronyism and black money was demonetisation which sent an unambiguous signal of the government's willingness to take risks in this important battle. In public perception, demonetisation was appreciated for its boldness and intent. The credibility of a broken system was restored.

None of this is reason for triumphalism. The battle against cronyism must continue. The effort to further liberalise the economy must be doubled. There is a long journey to traverse. The reform of government must continue to get special attention. However, it is clear that after the inflexion point of 2014, Modi has put India on the right track. Now, as growth recovers and heads back to levels of eight and nine per cent per annum, it will come with less cronyism and stable inflation. Therefore, it will be more sustainable. In the end, it will be transformative, for Modi has the right argument. Only a reoriented government, freer markets and individual participation, a unique public–private–personal partnership can lead India to prosperity. For once, India is on the right trajectory.